"With so much advice and guidance available related to the college experience, there is relatively little about the next step: finding your way to a satisfying career.

"Amy Feind Reeves's *College to Career, Explained* helps young people get started and find direction with a focus on linking skills and goals to jobs you'd actually enjoy.

"She offers detailed guidance on the tools and resources that underpin a successful job search, including how to develop resumes and cover letters that stand out; build and use a network; and successfully interview across a range of job types. Importantly, she also offers insights on the offer process and those early days of a new job.

"While a job search creates anxiety for most, Amy's practical tips and straight scoop—including on how hiring managers really think—help take the mystery out of the process.

"This book should be required reading for any college student, college career advisor or parent who wants to be well-prepared for this important launch point and ensure a strong start into the real world." — **NANCY LOTANE,** Chief Human Resources Officer, Bain Capital

"Amy is the real deal—both n   are lucky that she has turned her c   ill to job searching. Unlike other bo   ical, easy to read, and, most import   what employers and hiring managers want and presenting it in a way that college-age students and new graduates can understand. This

book is one that all college students and new graduates should have handy to prepare for an interview." — **MARK RANALLI,** CEO, BioSqueeze, Inc & former Dean, Jake Jabs College of Business and Entrepreneurship, Montana State University—Bozeman

"Amy has packed a lot of insight and direction into *College to Career, Explained* about what organizations are looking for from new professionals at every stage of the hiring process. She explains why and how we make decisions with clarity, using real-world examples. Following the instructions in this book will definitely increase your chances of getting hired regardless of your major and academic background." — **JOHN MARSHALL,** CEO of the Potential Energy Coalition and former President of the Princeton Review

"As a small business owner, finding applicants with the right skills and interviewing can be time-consuming and overwhelming. Amy's book is one of the most comprehensive on the market for teaching candidates how to prepare for and ace any interview. *College to Career, Explained* is definitely the book that any college senior or new grad should have in their arsenal" — **KRISTIN MARQUET,** Founder + Creative Director, Marquet Media LLC

COLLEGE TO CAREER,
Explained

TOOLS, SKILLS & CONFIDENCE
FOR YOUR JOB SEARCH

Amy Feind Reeves

Epigraph Books
Rhinebeck, New York

Paperback ISBN: 978-1-954744-75-2
eBook ISBN: 978-1-954744-76-9

Library of Congress Control Number: 2022911300

Book and cover design by Colin Rolfe

Epigraph Books
22 East Market Street, Suite 304
Rhinebeck, NY 12572
epigraphps.com

For my parents, Fred and Marge, who taught me life is to be enjoyed.
For my daughter, Mary, whom I enjoy most of all.
And for my husband, Doug, who believed I could do this.

Contents

PART II. DEVELOP TOOLS

PART IV. HIRED

Introduction

This book is the result of a long-held passion to help new college graduates avoid what I have come to think of as my Gap Year—the year after I graduated from college. Did I travel to exotic destinations? Work at a cool resort? Build memories that I still think back on with delight? No.

My Gap Year: I lay in bed for most of the first three months, then got a job as a secretary out of the *New York Times* classifieds (ask your parents) in a vaguely Dunder Mifflin-like office. I learned the hard way that even if you are smart, hardworking, and have a good GPA from a good college, you can fail at a career job search.

While I was working as an admin, I learned from my friends who had gotten the jobs that I wanted, what they were doing every day and how they had presented themselves to get hired. The following year, I got one of those jobs easily. (This is all in Chapter 1, by the way. You'll laugh. You'll cry.) Turns out I was good at that job and really liked the work. What was the difference from the year before? I didn't understand what the job was and I didn't understand how I could bring value to the role, and as a result, I had no idea what the hiring managers were looking for in a candidate.

Duh. Knocking the interview out of the park was not rocket science. I just didn't know how to do it before. I have been a keen student and teacher of that understanding ever since, and it has been, in more than one way, my profession: I was a hiring manager learning new industries for over twenty-five years. This book contains everything I have learned and is the resource I wish I had had way back when.

Figuring out what you want to do with your life professionally is a lot of pressure, can sneak up on you while you are busy doing other things, and comes with lots of unhelpful, unwanted advice. The good news is that the clear and common-sense advice presented here will open the door for you to a world of possibilities.

A couple of things to keep in mind:

- Finding your way professionally does not have to be left in the hands of fate. You can apply the structured approach presented here to identify what might be a good first job for you and how you can conduct a job search to get hired to do that job.
- The right opportunity will not magically appear on the horizon. You are going to need to do some work to understand what a good opportunity for you looks like and how to make that opportunity a reality.
- Don't feel pressured that you will be locked into a career path with your first or second job. Hardly anyone finds what they want to do for the rest of their life when they are twenty-two. However, pretty much everything you learn at this stage will be worthwhile in helping you figure things out down the line.

The tools laid out in this book are all based on my twenty-five-plus-years' experience as a hiring manager and ten-plus years as a career coach. They will provide you with what you need to get noticed and hired in today's workforce. And all the information is applicable to any job search in any industry. JobCoachAmy clients have been successful finding work in sports marketing, financial services, high-tech sales, start-ups of all sorts, management consulting, nonprofit management, and the NSA, to name just a few representative fields.

These tools include:

- An understanding of how you can add value to an organization
- Skills to research what jobs may be available to you
- A step-by-step guide for creating an effective résumé, cover letter, and elevator pitch
- Networking skills and advice
- Interview preparation guides that teach you what and how to understand what hiring managers want
- Tips for starting your new role on the right foot and common mistakes to avoid

You will find examples, exercises, and tutorials that will support your understanding of the material.

While free advice is everywhere, it is usually worth its price. You can find an abundance of free career advice in the form of less than seventy-five characters, jargon-laden blogs, and LinkedIn, Instagram, and TikTok posts—to name a few. But what you cannot find are the two things I provide you here:

1. An end-to-end, detailed understanding of the search process that provides strategies, tactics, and examples at every step
2. A focus on the needs of the two key players: you, the job seeker; and the person who will make the decision on whether to bring you in, the hiring manager

I've tried to make this book as fun and interesting as possible. My hope is that you will find work in general to be endlessly fun and interesting, and you should. If you don't find yourself in a role where you are enjoying most of your days, please come back to this book again. There is no reason not to find energy, engagement, and satisfaction in your work.

You don't need to be a recent college graduate or a first-time job seeker to learn from this book. My methodology has helped those in career transitions at all levels, those getting back into the workforce after a hiatus, and those simply interested in refining their knowledge about business, job searching, and interview skills.

Chapter 1.
A Few Things No One Ever Tells You

Let's get rid of that awful pit in your stomach that appears whenever you think about job searching.

In this chapter, I'm first going to tell you seven amazing and true facts no one ever tells you about the whole damned search process that are going to make you feel a lot better right off the bat, such as: many of the skills and experiences you have gained navigating the world to date are fully transferrable to the workplace *and* to your résumé. Are you very well organized? (Hello, lovers of office supplies! Turns out all those planners and stickies were an investment in a salable skill.) Do you get along with just about everyone? (Social butterflies, I now deem you to be excellent at relationship development.) Are you able to stay calm under pressure? (Didn't get the internship and waited tables instead? Rejoice!)

Then, we'll do a deep dive into one of the primo Amazing Facts About Job Searching: Everyone has been where you are right now. After that, I'll explain why my experience as a hiring manager is uniquely valuable for you. (Yes, you'll come across recruiters and human resource business partners in your search—however, the hiring manager is the key decision-maker and your key audience.) And I'll explain why the advice you'll find here is unique and can be used in conjunction with any additional advice you find. Then we'll get on with learning the mechanics of the process that will be less awful and (who knows?) maybe even enlightening and fun.

Seven Amazing Facts about Job Searching

There are at least seven amazing and absolutely true facts about job searching that no one ever tells you. Let's crowd out the noise and the anxiety you have about starting your career by focusing on your favorite subject: you!

My job as an author and a coach is to treat you professionally and give you the all the benefits my clients enjoy. But I should warn you that my coaching style includes what my clients, colleagues, and friends often refer to as my "Jersey side": I will interrupt myself occasionally to show you and deliver a little (important!) tough love.

JerseyCoachAmy: *The quickest route to living in a cupboard under the stairs is to wait for a magical letter to be delivered with your job offer. Not going to happen. Do a little work.*

Amazing Fact 1. You already have the experience you need to succeed in a job.

If you've gotten to the point where you've succeeded in life by some measure, you've got the experience to excel in a work setting (and most likely, multiple settings) that will give you a paycheck.

There are a lot of similarities between succeeding in life and succeeding in a job. Here is a short list of some characteristics that you may possess that are highly desirable to hiring managers:

- Being well-organized

- Getting along well with other people
- Holding up under pressure
- Hustling to meet deadlines
- Demonstrating good judgment
- Having a good work ethic
- Working well independently but also knowing when to ask for help
- Taking initiative to solve problems when they arise
- Contributing to teamwork
- Ability to see the big picture but also pay attention to the details

Even if you have never had a full-time job, you have probably demonstrated many of these skills in an academic setting, part-time job, internship, community volunteer role, or even in a campus role, such as a campus party planner. More importantly, you probably have a story that illustrates your skills. I have never had a client who, when pressed, was not able to come with an example that they thought was pretty ordinary, but I knew was interview gold for demonstrating their potential to be an outstanding employee. For example:

Client View	JobCoachAmy View
"I taught at the same camp for ten summers, so I have no real job experience."	This shows people liked you at that camp enough to invite you back for ten straight years! This means you were a good employee, got along well with people, and probably were given increasing responsibility every year. Talk about demonstrated relationship development skills, work ethic, and a track record of accountability! This is a really positive thing.

Client View	JobCoachAmy View
"Twice I was asked by my sorority to run our campus-wide blood drive. But the blood drive was only a sorority thing."	This was campus-wide, so several thousand students were involved, and you were asked to run the blood drive twice, so the first time must have been successful. This is a big project that requires marketing to get the students there, logistics for getting parking permits for the bus or cars, getting snacks and beverages there on time, creating incentives and rewards for blood donors, and maybe even some entertainment for people waiting in line? This is a great example of successful project management! Include on your résumé the number of people who went each year, examples of details that needed to be managed, the number of people on your team, your budget (if any), and known outcomes. For example, how many people came through? Did all run smoothly? Did you have a goal you met or came close to meeting? It's okay that the event was for a sorority or other campus organization, prospective employers care about your abilities. Even if you don't want to mention the sponsoring group, *do* mention the project.

Client View	JobCoachAmy View
"I had a part-time campus job working for the athletic director."	This must have required setting up and taking down chairs for events, logging in scores and statistics from various teams on the road and sending them to campus media outlets, handling score boards during home games, preparing for weather issues on the field, and a lot of other details. This shows a track record for attention to detail, project management, ability to juggle a lot of tasks at the same time, and ability to meet deadlines.

Amazing Fact 2. (Almost) everyone has been where you are right now. Most want to help you—you just need to make helping you easy for them.

Very few people in this world step out of school into their dream job (even if your mother seems to know of a lot of them). Just about everyone with whom you network and interview has had the experience of:

- not knowing what they want to do;
- worrying that they will become the only person in the history of their family, group of friends, or college alumni that never gets a job without a nametag or hairnet—ever;
- feeling that a career is like the Great and Powerful Oz: completely scary and totally hidden.

Most people want to help you through this stressful time in life. The trick is to learn how to make helping you easy for them. You will see as you go through this book's step-by-step guide that it's not nearly as difficult as you may think. You just need to develop a little insight into yourself about what you like doing, then combine that with a little knowledge about the job search process. From there, you can figure out how the things you like doing can be translated into a salable skill and use that information to make it easy for others to help you meet your goals.

For example:

Like working with spreadsheets and data? Let people know you are interested in quantitative analysis.

Enjoy looking at new products when they come out in drug stores, retail outlets or grocery stores? You may want to learn more about consumer-packaged goods careers, maybe brand management or category management (look it up).

Know that you don't want to sit at a desk all day? You may be interested in real estate, or a career where you are traveling to do sales or perhaps compliance work.

By the time you are ready to talk to people to ask for guidance you will have learned enough through this book to make providing guidance easy for them. Then later, when you are ready to ask for introductions and interviews, you will be even more precise and prepared.

JerseyCoachAmy: *Don't be an idiot. If someone offers to help you start your career, don't expect them to figure out how. Meet them at least halfway by explaining what kind of job you want. You could also simply ask what kind of entry level roles are available at their company. Alternatively, or additionally, ask who they know that works for a company who hires entry level roles. Can you speak with that person? This is not rocket science, people. Just use a little common sense.*

Amazing Fact 3. You can't know what you don't know, but you can learn it.

Imagine you've never taken a trip on a plane before. Think about how much you'd need to know and find out, such as:

- Ticket prices vary significantly based on how, when, and where you buy your ticket.
- Security checks require some things to be removed from your bags at screening and others to be left at home entirely.
- Checked luggage is taken away by airline and airport staff. Where does your luggage go? After you arrive at the next airport, how do you get your luggage back?

These are just a few of the details that seasoned travelers know and do on autopilot after a while. But if you've never traveled before, how do you even know what questions to ask? And if you've never traveled, what isn't a seemingly dumb question? Now flip roles: What if you *are* an experienced air traveler? Where and how would you start explaining it all to the uninitiated?

Job searching is similar in that you need to know some basic rules and expectations and after the first couple of times out, you'll get the hang of it.

Hardly anyone gets a thorough, end-to-end explanation about the basics of a job search *or* about airline travel. As a result, these tasks seem more daunting and complex than they actually are to anyone who has never done them before. But they are both easily navigable with the right guidance and a little practice.

Once you understand how a hiring manager thinks, your job search will become a very different endeavor. Like airline travel, job search-ing can still be frustrating. But practice once or twice and suddenly, the process is not so scary. Suddenly, the whole thing makes sense.

Amazing Fact 4. Your job search doesn't have to be awful.

Your job search can be energizing and fun. Networking can expand your circle of contacts and help you clarify your goals. You can learn all kinds of things that you would never have otherwise known. You may even surprise yourself.

Learning about what people do can be really interesting if you keep a good attitude and stay open-minded and engaged. Thinking about what you like doing and what you are good at is a very valuable exercise both now and in the future.

As your knowledge of yourself and the job market becomes more sophisticated, you'll know how to revisit and revise your plan. Understanding what jobs are out there and how to get them is a life skill that you can learn once, then use, and even teach others, for the rest of your life.

All the work you will do—from résumé building, to networking, to thank you notes—is worthwhile. Careers are long, and industries are small. The person interviewing you today could be the person you interview to work for you in a few years. Sound crazy? You would be surprised.

> **JerseyCoachAmy:** *Don't be a jerk. Ever. Be rude to the receptionist, and they may mention it to the hiring manager at the coffee station (I would) and* it will matter. *Snub the interviewer you suspect dinged you when you see them in a local supermarket, and I guarantee they will either be at the next cookout you attend or will start working at your next company.*

Similarly, the person you contact through the friend of a friend for an informational network interview may end up working for you someday—and they know it. This happens more often than you think.

Don't feel like you don't have anything to offer in return because one day, you likely will. Be bold. Just be sure to circle back eventually and let everyone who spoke with you know where you have landed once your search ends. It's not a hard thing to do, but surprisingly, most people fail at this.

Why is circling back important? When you talk to someone once, it's likely because they are within someone else's network. When you follow up after a talk, that person becomes part of your network.

Amazing Fact 5. The only thing you can do wrong is to do nothing.

You can leverage your status as a career novice or career explorer to have all kinds of interesting conversations and experiences that will influence the rest of your life. For new grads and other job seekers, the worst thing you can do is nothing. The best thing you can do is to have a good attitude and start asking questions.

Ask a question of someone you respect about how they got started in their career.

Go to indeed.com and just type in the words "entry-level" or your major and the city you want to live in and read what comes back.

See the career office at your school, whether you are a current student or an alum.

Do one thing, then another. Each time will be less scary, and each time you will learn something. Pretty soon, you will have an answer to the dreaded "How is your job search going?" question.

Amazing Fact 6. There are always good jobs for good people.

It is easy to get discouraged, and if you need to take a breather for a few days, go ahead. But there are always good jobs for good people. Believe in yourself and what you have to offer, and you will get interviews and eventually, a job.

You only need one job. If there is a downturn in the economy, that is not an excuse to be discouraged or to stop trying. Whenever there is a downturn somewhere in the economy, there is an upturn somewhere else.

For example, if there is an increase in crime, security systems sales grow and hire more people to keep up with that growth. If the economy is stalled because people are generally spending less, products that help save money experience growth in response. Similarly, there are always individual companies that can beat an industry downturn.

Even within industries and companies that are suffering, there is always employee turnover: people get sick or retire, companies cut employees who aren't performing or who have been garnering bigger salaries than they deserve, or companies just plain want to decrease headcount in one area so that they can add headcount in another area.

Amazing Fact 7. People turn themselves down for jobs way more often than recruiters or hiring managers.

It is a well-known fact that you miss 100 percent of the swings you don't take at bat. This is true for job searching as well as baseball. I find most people talk themselves out of applying for jobs before they even get to bat. Every client I have ever worked with can bypass a job after reading the job description just once:

- "The commute would not be great."
- "I really don't know enough about the industry."
- "There is someone who works there I don't like, so I probably would not like working there."

Well, the commute might be worse, but the work and the pay might be amazing. You don't know yet! If you don't know enough about the industry, you can learn. And if there is someone there you don't like, it's possible that nobody there likes them either! My point is that you should always apply. What's the worst that could happen? They never call. So what?

The bottom line is you need to be accountable for your own future and not let anyone convince you your own future, is out of your control. You also need to be accountable to yourself and be open to every opportunity. You never know.

JerseyCoachAmy: *For the love of God, give yourself a chance at success by taking a shot at success. There is never going to be an UberCareers that delivers a job the way that UberEats delivers a dozen donuts. I mean, salads. You're going to have to get off the couch, call some people, and apply for a lot of jobs. You'll only need one.*

It's Important to Commit to Your Search

Even with clear guidance, finding a career will take time, commitment, and patience. If you want to go to Europe or drive cross-country for a year, do it. If you want to spend some time as a ski or tennis bum, go for it. If you're not quite sure you are ready to leave the job you have, stay.

Here's what you cannot do:

- Be half-hearted about your search
- Wait around for something to come to you
- Fake it by claiming you are doing job research when you are actually going to the gym, binging on social media or playing video games
- Get stuck because you don't know where to begin

Everyone Has Been Where You Are: My Story

To back up my claim that everyone has been where you are, here's my deal: late last century, I graduated from a good liberal arts college with a respectable GPA, campus leadership experience, and a couple of moderately interesting, but well-paying, temp roles on my résumé. My fellow classmates were flocking to Wall Street training programs, so that was where I figured I would go as well. "How hard could getting a job be?" I thought.

A few months after graduation, I watched my friends take their empty briefcases off to their first days of work while I remained jobless. I was crushed, miserable, and in utter disbelief that for the first time in my life I had been a complete failure at something—a job search at which I had worked hard and done everything I had been told to do. And I had great skirt suits! I had no idea where to turn, nor did my family or friends who wanted to help but didn't know how.

Ultimately, I accepted the best paying job I could find as an administrative assistant and started processing my experience and asking questions. What did my friends actually do in their jobs? What did their bosses do? What were my friends learning on the job? What skills did they learn in college that they were applying to their job?

Slowly, I started to understand that these jobs were supporting larger teams who, in turn, were chasing goals. Once the bigger picture became clear, I began to understand how the skills I had developed in college would allow me to contribute to those teams and goals. I understood I was a less attractive candidate because I did not have a background in math or economics, but I came up with a strategy to work around that fact. I read all I could about banking and accounting, and I learned all I could about corporate-finance trends in the *Wall Street Journal* and the *New York Times*. I learned from my friends what questions to expect during an interview and prepared my answers in advance.

By the following spring, I'd landed a bank training program role at the first place I interviewed and found that not only did I enjoy what I was doing, but that I was also good at it.

How had I been so bad at interviewing for a job after college but was really good at it a year later?

The answer is actually pretty simple: Job searching and interviewing, like anything else, is a learned skill. The process doesn't necessarily favor the smart or the hard-working. The process favors those who understand how it works and how performance is measured. And like any process, it can be learned.

My passion, since that miserable summer late last century, has been to support and guide job seekers who are blindly navigating unfamiliar waters. The intention of this book is to take the fear out of the process, and replace that fear with specific strategies, tactics, and tools that readers can use to find a job they want and get hired to do it.

Still today, as when I graduated college, there are few really good resources for job seekers who don't have industry connections. Still today, candidates often arrive for interviews either sorely unprepared or are freakishly prepared in an irrelevant way.

Many people don't stray far from their parents' professions. Others don't want to be anywhere near their parents' professions and get stuck, or head to graduate school and get stuck a few years later.

No one really seems to know what people do outside of their general area of expertise. (More on that later.) Advice will come from a variety of sources, both solicited and unsolicited, and can run the gamut from disparate to conflicting, and it may or may not be actionable.

What The Deal Is with Hiring Managers
(and Why Knowing This Matters So Much!)

What makes my method, approach, and tools different from those found in any other source out there is that they focus on the two important players:

1. You, and
2. The hiring manager who will ultimately decide whether to give you a job.

You, obviously, know why *you* are important.

The hiring manager, in case you don't know, is the end customer of all the recruiters and human resource professionals and potential colleagues involved in the overall hiring process. The hiring manager, and the hiring manager alone, is the one who makes the call on which candidates are or are not worthy of the budget allocation earmarked to pay the given salary. Here's the deal:

1. The hiring manager needs to meet specific goals.
2. To do that, the hiring manager goes to bat for headcount (i.e., the number of skilled people needed to reach that goal). Each skilled person fills a role which requires a salary, and the sum total of those salaries is his or her headcount budget. You are interviewing for the budget allocated to your potential role.
3. The hiring manager needs to believe that you are someone who can solidly contribute to the team to meet or exceed their goals.
4. If a goal is not met, the hiring manager's job is on the line.

Not very mysterious, right?

My methodology is based on the simple premise that you need to do three things to impress the hiring manager enough to prove you are worth that budgeted salary. This applies to *any* role you may interview for:

1. Explain why you want this job—as specifically as possible, and with as many examples as possible.
2. Describe the skills you have that will allow you to do the job well—link what you understand will be required of/in the job to

specific skills and experience you have. This should also include examples.

3. Show that you want the job! The job always goes to the person who wants the job the most, and it's easy to spot when someone is authentically enthusiastic and when they are just going through the motions because they want the offer but not necessarily the job. And here's a tough truth: Forget about waiting to be enthusiastic in your thank-you note after the interview—the decision of whether or not to hire you will have usually been made by that point.

How can I be so sure of all this? I developed in-depth understanding of how organizations work, and what roles exist in them, after many years as a management consultant, entrepreneur, and executive across a wide range of industries. I have been fortunate, over a long time in the workforce, to have a solid understanding of what people do within organizations and what makes those people successful, or not successful, in those jobs. My varied career has given me insight not only into hiring practices, but also into the nature of what jobs are available across industries.

This book offers you a unique perspective and a set of directions for what you need to know and do throughout the job search from beginning to successful end. When you build these tools for yourself, you are building on my decades of experience as a hiring manager and job coach. You should build on this foundation with other counselors, advisors, and authors, but build your foundation first.

College career counselors will be helpful to you, so sign up early and often. If you can, try to find one with a background in the workforce, not in other college career centers. Your alumni and/or Handshake database username and password are essential. Look for social media, blogs, and books that make sense to you, but don't go out there without the tools I'm giving you here. There are a tremendous number of resources out there, but there is also a great deal of noise: you'll find conflicting advice, the afore-mentioned free advice that is worth the zero price it's offered for, and sales pitches to job seekers that come disguised as free advice. Arm yourself with what you find here first.

Authors who offer human resource credentials or millennial counseling experience can offer great ideas. However, this advice tends to focus on *one aspect* of the job search (e.g., interviewing, networking, or keeping your spirits up) and not the *entire* process. Those are important topics, and I encourage you to find any resources beyond what I have written here that can be helpful to you. But plug that advice into the framework provided here to best leverage where in the process the advice is meant to help.

At the core of the job search process is the goal of finding a job where you will do something you are good at and enjoy. In the next chapter, we'll identify what you are good at that provides value for companies.

On Procrastination and The Great Resignation[1]

Beginning in early 2021, the US and other parts of the world began to see a paradoxical trend in employment: workers voluntarily resigning in great numbers, even though the underlying economic fundamentals did not suggest a strong reason for it. With unemployment low, you may be thinking this means there are a lot of great jobs available for you to step right into. You can kick back, relax and pretty much wait for the jobs to come to you.

Maybe, not so much.

I'm not going to try to analyze why this pattern has occurred or what it means for underlying market fundamentals or long-term structural changes that need to occur in the corporate world.

---

[1] "The great resignation is coming," says Anthony Klotz, an associate professor of management at Texas A&M University who's studied the exits of hundreds of workers." Arianne Cohen, "How to Quit Your Job in the Great Post-Pandemic Resignation Boom," *Bloomberg*, May,10,2021, archived and retrieved from the original on July 8, 2021, *Ready to say adios to your job? You're not alone.*

> **JerseyCoachAmy:** *I do have a few thoughts.*

Personally, I think it is going to be a while before we get a handle on the seismic shifts that have happened in the world since the COVID pandemic started and what they will mean for us going forward. But what does it mean for *you* entering the job market? You are likely wondering, and you definitely have relatives who will ask. Following is my *opinion* of the impact that The Great Resignation will have on your job search:

- *You may have a greater number of opportunities for entry-level type roles.* In my anecdotal experience, a lot of resignations have occurred because in recent years when employees left roles through regular attrition they were not replaced, as a cost-saving measure on the part of the organization. This left remaining workers with two times, or even three times, their former workload. This caused frustration, burnout and quitting. I think employers will continue to push for reduced salary expense. But instead of doing business with fewer employees they will try to do it with greater numbers of lower-salaried employees, interns, and contractors. That means, potentially, more entry-level roles for you. Some companies are starting to invest again in training programs and development for entry-level professionals.
- *A greater number of entry-level roles available will not necessarily translate into you having an easier time getting one of them.* Hiring a new employee is expensive, and hiring a new employee who does not work out is *really* expensive. For the kind of job you want, companies are not going to lower their hiring standards during a labor shortage. They are still going to want someone who really understands what they are getting into, someone who has a really good chance of doing well in the role by having exhibited the skills required, and someone who has demonstrated a

strong interest in the field. In other words, don't stop reading at this point.

- *Yes, this is a good time to enter the job market—in theory.* It is always good to having timing on your side in a job search. Talent and perseverance are also really good allies. And you don't have to have all three to land a job that you want and will make you happy. But in almost all cases, you need two of the three. Don't procrastinate about starting your search because you think that timing is going to be enough.

JerseyCoachAmy: *"Economic fundamentals and statistics are so good for job seekers!", say lots of people who are not going to give you a paycheck. Figure out your fundamentals. Don't worry about the country's.*

Summary

- Everyone has been where you are, including me. You're going to come out the other side. It's easy to fall into the trap of believing that you totally screwed up because you studied the wrong thing, because you haven't worked hard enough inside or outside of school, because you're not interesting enough, or because you don't have a clue as to what you want to do with the next phase of your life. Don't let yourself go there.
- Every aspect of getting a job and being good at that job can be learned more easily than you think. If you are generally a successful human, you can be successful at this.
- If you have generally been a successful human, you have skills and examples of those skills that you can leverage to get and do well in interviews. This book will show you how.
- If you are going to follow the step-by-step course of action laid

out in this book, you are going to need to commit to it. If you can't/ aren't going to commit to this right now, then put this book, and any ideas you have about going through the motions, away until you are ready. My methodology only works if you commit to it.

There will be lots of job search advice available to you. Be wary of the source. Some of the free advice you find and receive is worth the cost. Other specific advice—that comes from your college career office, a recent alum with a job similar to what you want, or someone in the profession you want who is willing to help you—is invaluable. In general, my hope is that the advice in this book should not conflict with anything you learn from another source, as it is more detailed and tactical. Use your own judgment about what feels right.

PART I
Develop Focus

Chapter 2

Link Your Skills and Interests to an Objective

Hopefully you are starting to think about your job search with a little more excitement and a little less dread. If not, don't worry. We still have a lot of runway. In this chapter we're going to keep focusing on you (yay!), and I'm going to explain how the skills you've already acquired can be used to build your story. I'm not talking about accounting or Python, although those are certainly salable skills. I'm talking about life skills, like getting along well with people or being able to balance conflicting priorities. In this chapter I am going to explain how you can identify, package, and present these skills so that they become shining attributes to potential hiring managers.

Doing the exercises in this chapter will help you to

- identify what you want to do, based on your interests,
- identify what you have to offer, based on your skills, and
- explain how these two things have led you to choose a particular interest area / role.

These are really the three most important things you need to be able to articulate. Why? Because when you ultimately get into an interview, you are going to need to prove that you

- understand what you would be doing in the job,
- can do the job, and
- want the job.

Sound familiar? If you read the introduction, you saw those three bullet points before, and you will see them again. We'll return to these three concepts[1] again and again throughout the book. The work we'll do in this chapter will help build what you ultimately create to say in your interviews to support all three of those bullet points.

Define Your Interests and Your Skills

The first half of this exercise will help you translate what you enjoy doing and feel confident doing into marketable skills. The second half will help you summarize what you have learned in a way that makes it clear to networking contacts and potential employers how you can add value.

Exercise 1: Three Lists

- Write down the names of five to ten companies where you would like to work and ten jobs you think you could do for them.
- Write down five to ten things you know you are good at doing, and create examples.
- Write down five to ten things you really enjoy doing.

Don't censor yourself while completing this exercise. Enjoy shopping online for bargains? That shows an interest in conducting research to support decision-making. Like cooking? This could indicate an affinity for project work: you line up your ingredients and your tools then work

---

[1] If you work in consulting long enough, or at least longer than a decade as I did, you think of all concepts in threes. It's a thing.

to perfect the results under what can often be a short, crucial timeline. If you want it, if you are good at, if you enjoy it, write it down.

There is a worksheet for this exercise in the accompanying workbook, also available from on my site, www.jobcoachamy.com/downloads.

Below is an example of a former client, Elaine. Elaine was a Spanish major and taught Spanish during the summers. But she came to me because she wanted to find an agency or marketing role that would allow her to continue to apply and deepen her knowledge of Spanish language and culture.

Here is Elaine's first list.

Companies I'd Like to Work for and What I Would Like to Do:

1. Zara
   - Choose what clothes go into various stores in the US
   - Decide how to market clothes differently in different countries
   - Write ad campaigns in Spanish
   - Research ways to promote the brand
2. Univision
   - Use social media to promote the brand
   - Write for the website
   - Help decide and negotiate what ad campaigns will be shown during shows
3. Telemundo
   - Use social media to promote the brand
   - Write for the website
   - Help decide and negotiate what ad campaigns will be shown during shows
   - Develop social media content for the VOCES Edition of the Huffington Post
   - Report/research lifestyle stories for different areas of the paper edition of VOCES

4. Buzzfeed (Spain version)
   - Report/research features for different areas of the paper
   - Write lifestyle features, tell personal stories
5. Unilever
   - Write ads for multicultural marketing to the Latino community
   - Research and collect information on different demographics within Hispanic communities
6. Pepsi
   - Write ads for multicultural marketing to the Latino community
   - Research and collect information on different demographics within Hispanic communities
7. Avon
   - Write ads for multicultural marketing to the Latino community
   - Research and collect information on different demographics within Hispanic communities
8. FIFA
   - Help players get acclimated to different cultures—players moving from the United States to Hispanic countries or vice versa
9. ESPN
   - Help players get acclimated to different cultures—players moving from the United States to Hispanic countries or vice versa

A couple of clear themes emerged here:

- She wants to leverage her knowledge of Spanish culture.
- She is interested in pop culture, particularly sports and fashion.
- She is drawn to the idea of how brands are built and how different strategies may be needed for different demographics.

- She has confidence in her writing abilities.

She then listed ten things she knew she was good at and included examples for each:

Ten Things I Know I Do Well:

1. Proactive about identifying what needs to get done and completing required tasks, often under tight deadlines

Examples:
   - Creating lesson plans without direct guidance
   - Teaching myself required technology skills, such as creating PowerPoint presentations

2. Juggling a number of demands at once

Examples:
   - Maintained a good GPA while holding down a twenty-hour-a-week, part-time job during the school year
   - Spent junior year abroad and learned to study in a foreign language while adapting to a foreign culture
   - Worked as teacher, mentor, administrator, and curriculum developer at a prestigious academic summer camp

3. Ability to break down complex goals into a series of straightforward tasks

Examples:
   - Developing daily lesson plans from high level achievement criteria
   - Creating research methodologies to support my thesis, and efficiently segment out useful/actionable data
   - Explaining complex concepts to students by breaking them down into clear ideas and examples

4. Keeping in contact with people
Example:

- Still keep in constant contact with friends from home and with international friends

5. Making lesson plans and PowerPoints.
Examples:

- Informative presentations that are interesting to students and comply with timing restrictions

6. Working under pressure
Example:

- I often need to come up with lesson plans fifteen minutes before class.

7. Multitasking
Example:

- I had to wear many hats as a Spanish teacher during the summer: monitor students away from home for the first time, mentor them academically and socially, perform administrative work.

8. Explaining difficult concepts to students
Example:

- Taking information that might have been over their heads and breaking the information down into simple concepts so that they would be able to understand the material

9. Working efficiently and quickly
Example:

- While teaching, able to correct and grade quickly and efficiently so that students would have their work back in a timely fashion

10. Creative

Example:

- Innovative in developing lesson plans and strategies with students to keep them interested and stimulated by the material

Lastly, Elaine listed things that she *enjoys* doing and *why*. Odds are you already know what you like doing (e.g., doing make up, working with spreadsheets, organizing your fraternity rush). You want to write these things down so that you can consider the implications that they might have for jobs you would likely enjoy (e.g., buyer for Sephora, digital response analyst, project manager).

Here's Elaine's last list.

Ten Things I Like Doing and Why:

1. Online shopping—
Why? It's interesting to look at how different things are presented on websites and/or finding different deals.

2. Yoga and running—
Why? Hard but rewarding exercise is physically and mentally relaxing; a good workout gives me the chance to process things.

3. Learning about new cultures and languages—
Why? I like learning about how different communities of people see or do things differently, and how language changes based on different dialects or sounds.

4. Traveling—
Why? I like being able to explore new things and take in different kinds of experiences for the first time.

5. Cooking—

Why? I like being creative using different recipes with new foods. I also enjoy figuring out how to make good meals while still eating healthy.

6. Keeping up with social media and trends—
Why? I like following all social media outlets to keep up with friends and celebrities, and spot new trends.

7. Going out with friends—
Why? I like being social and keeping up my relationships with friends while having fun.

8. Trying new things—
Why? I don't want to get in too much of a rut, and I always can appreciate the value of something new.

9. Writing—
Why? I like compiling and expressing my thoughts, whether what I'm writing is for school (students, parents, administrators) or a research paper, or if I'm using writing as a creative outlet for myself.

10. Research—
Why? I always enjoyed this aspect of college. I particularly enjoyed identifying a wide range of sources from which to pull material—both online and analog sources.

What can Elaine learn about her interests as they relate to the professional world from this exercise?

- She enjoys things that require hard work and discipline (yoga and running) that have a payoff.
- She is creative, as shown by her interest in writing, cooking, exploring new media outlets, and watching social media evolve. She would likely be good at problem solving, but there is not a

lot to indicate she would enjoy working with spreadsheets or numbers.

- She is adventurous: she loves travel and trying new things. This probably means she is pretty well organized and also always on the lookout for what is new. This may mean a job that involves research about what is new and what is trending in a particular field would be fun for her.

- The fact that she enjoys keeping up with friends and social media means she is probably going to be happy in a role where she has some social interaction. A job where she is at her desk all day without any group projects or spending time with colleagues will likely not make her happy.

What skills show up in these exercises that are interesting to employers?

- The fact that Elaine is a yoga enthusiast (where you practice peacefulness) who enjoys traveling (which is not for the anxious) indicates she is well suited to work in in high-pressure situations. This can be a lead discussion and résumé point. However, that point needs an example to back it up. For Elaine, it's her track record as a summer-camp teacher. Teacher/counselors have a demanding role: the kids need supervision all the time and you are always "on."

- Learning new cultures indicates an intellectual curiosity, another thing that employers want and is something that, frankly, cannot be taught. It's valuable because having intellectual curiosity can be the difference between an employee who is interested in finding the solution to a problem on their own and one who will say "I've taken this as far as I can, you figure it out from here."

- Teaching requires significant organization skills and time management. One aspect: you need to plan what you want to get across in a limited time. Adding "well organized" to the headline of Elaine's résumé would be easily defensible and attract potential employers.

- Her writing skills would be valuable in any environment. When companies seek this skill set, it often shows up in job descriptions as "excellent written and verbal communication skills" or "requires strong written communication skills." Whether this requirement shows up or not, communication skills are highly desirable in any role. Elaine has a history of writing and enjoys it personally. This is something she can leverage to her advantage.
- Running is hard work. You can put these kinds of hobbies in the "Personal" section of your resume, and employers will get the idea that if you are not lazy outside of work, you are likely not lazy at work either.

Working through this exercise yourself will help you think through your interests and skills into an overall picture of you,and will serve as the foundation for understanding how you can link your interests to your skills, and later, your skills to a career objective.

Don't be shy about drawing on all your life experiences to date: part-time jobs, campus activities, group projects, volunteer works, and your academic career. They all matter. Did you take a full course load while holding down a thirty-hour-a-week job at Target? That requires a lot of time-management skills and the ability to juggle multiple priorities simultaneously. Any employer will welcome those skills.

Link Your Skills to an Objective

Now that you have spent some time thinking about the kinds of things you like to do and the kinds of things you are good at doing, let's translate those into an objective for your job search. The goal of this next exercise is to give you answers to the questions "What do you want to do?" and "Why?" You have some clear examples available in the form of the lists you just created. These will become the basis of your elevator pitch—a critical tool that we'll cover in more depth later in Chapter 7.

Here is how Elaine translated her three lists into her job search objective.

Objective: "What Do You Want to Do?"

- Use my strong research and writing abilities
- Leverage my Spanish language skills and knowledge of Latin culture

Review your lists and work to boil the points down into something similarly cogent. For example:

- Add value with my written and verbal communication skills
- Work in a detail-oriented role due to enjoying keeping track of budget and other planning details
- Start in a role where I can be rewarded for my ability to get along well with people and build relationships
- Leverage the lab skills I gained tracking, collecting, and analyzing data

JerseyCoachAmy: *There is a connection between the things you like doing and what you will do at work. So don't be a dumbass. What do I mean by that? Well, if you hated your statistics and political science classes, for example, it will not be super fun for you to work in investments. In investments, you are constantly tracking statistical changes in the value of various financial instruments relative to other variables: time, interest rates, asset classes, blah, blah, blah. As for political science, that is about analyzing "whys": Why did this country move toward this political movement at this point in time? Why did* *this region's natural resources influence the state legislature's economic agenda before, but not now? Why, why, why? In investing, once you've identified the mathematical movements of investments, you need to identify the "why" of those movements. All in an effort, of course, to predict the future of investments. So, why would you want to go into a business where you would do two things* all day *that you know for sure* you don't like doing?

Three things to keep in mind:

1. **Think broadly and not literally.** I once had a client who told me they did an analysis with their assigned Ivy League career advisor who asked them what they enjoyed doing. They answered they enjoyed putting together furniture from Ikea. The advisor told them they should apply at IKEA once they received their $400K degree. I suggested they look for very detailed work that allowed them to work independently; they are very happy working in a life sciences lab now.

2. **Don't be judgmental.** What you enjoy doing is likely analogous to a salable skill. Are you the friend people come to when they need their bike fixed? You are probably skilled at taking the initiative to do what needs to be done. Are you a reliable morning running partner? You are likely highly responsible.

3. **Do not discount the things that make up who you are or overcommit to something you feel you "should" be.** If you know you will be miserable working at a desk forty hours a week, make peace with that fact now. You will save yourself countless hours of heartache and misery in the future. More importantly, you will not hurt your opportunity to make a good living for yourself. People who are the most successful make the most of what

they've got. People who try to be what someone else thinks they should be rarely become successful in their careers or their lives.

Go back to the lists you created and look for themes. Here are a few more sample themes where you may recognize yourself based on what you have written.

My job search objective is to

- work with large amounts of data, analyzing patterns to spot trends;
- use my persuasive abilities to generate sales;
- take my organizational capabilities and use them to manage complex projects like commercial construction or technology integration;
- use my energy to work in a fast-paced environment where I know I do well under pressure, such as a highly pressured sales environment where teams need to meet quotas, or in technology services where minimizing downtime is critical;
- take my coding or accounting/math or life science or other hard skill and put it to work in a work environment where I can see tangible the benefits/results of my efforts;
- work on a team to help keep an environment or a project running smoothly, and respond to requests, manage tasks, and keep people well informed;
- leverage my ability to keep track of and manage a lot of details.

Of course, if you know the place or industry you want, you should absolutely add that to this objective, such as

- in a marketing agency,
- in commercial real estate,

- for an online retailer,
- in the hospitality industry,
- or the like.

You can also add where you would like to work:

- in New York,
- in Paris,
- in Chicago, or
- in Wausau, Indiana.

But my point is that you don't have to start with a job or an industry. You need to start with what you like and enjoy doing. Then add the rest.

Timing

So, the only thing you could come up with for the last exercise is that you want to bake brownies and vacuum, are good at making brownies and vacuuming, and enjoy eating brownies while vacuuming? Don't feel bad.

You may feel that everyone else is getting ahead of you in a way that you may never be able to catch up. But life is long, and hard work has a way of finding its way to a reward. I used to keep a Gary Larsen cartoon framed in my tiny New York apartment as I was making my way up in the world from being a Wellesley-educated administrative assistant while most of my friends were hitting their strides in the worlds of finance or advertising or graduate school. The cartoon showed a mutt sitting in a convertible waving to the crowds gathered at a ticker-tape parade. The caption said, "Every Dog Has His Day." And in my experience, every dog does.

It's okay if you need some time to make brownies and vacuum. Just don't make a career of staying home. Getting started can seem overwhelming, but as previously stated, the worst thing you can do is nothing. If this focus-finding exercise doesn't work for you, find something that does.

Keep following the exercises in this book so you know how to research what is available and how to best talk to people about jobs.

Or make your own job based on a need you see.

Or take a job that doesn't stretch you in any way but keeps you busy.

Or help someone out who needs it—either in their business or personally. The work doesn't have to rock the earth, and it can be just for now. You never know what may come of helping someone else, and staying busy is always a good idea.

Also, don't feel pressure to figure out the rest of your life right now. Whenever you do this exercise, know that it will have an expiration date. What you like doing and are good at doing today is not necessarily what you are going to like doing and be good at doing in five years or maybe even in two years. You will likely change careers at least once, and in all likelihood, more than once in your life. There is no crystal ball that can tell you what job will make you happy in the future. But you do need to start somewhere figuring it out, and starting with things you know you like doing and are good at doing right now is as good a place as any.

On Freds

Let's consider, for a moment, my cousin whom I will call Fred. (In point of fact, his name is Fred.) Cousin Fred is disciplined and smart, worked hard in school and at his profession, and became successful by any measure. His unflagging work ethic has made his life personally and professionally rich. He is kind, knowledgeable, charming, and generous. He has known what he wanted to do his entire life, having probably found his focus sometime around middle school. Fred has had one job in his entire thirty-year career. In short, Fred is *not* what one would call "normal."

It is unnerving to know that Freds exist (kind of like when I go shopping and realize that if clothing manufacturers *make* size double-zeros, there must be actual people that *fit into* those clothes). But here's the thing about Freds:

- They are extremely rare, even though sometimes it may feel like everyone else is on the Fred path, except you.
- Even within the rarefied Fred sphere, not everyone becomes my cousin Fred—and *that* is what gives the rest of us hope.

Here's the classic Fred model:

Step 1. Work really hard and do well in school.

Step 2. Get a great job in a career that is meaningful, challenging, and rewarding.

Step 3. Work very, very hard for a very, very long time.

Step 4: Earn a big payout and enjoy life to the fullest.

Works every time, right? This is a set formula, right? And one you have to follow? Not so much.

- There are plenty of people who skip Steps 1 and 2 but make it to Step 4:
  - *Steve Jobs, Dolly Parton, Mark Zuckerberg.*
- There are plenty of people who complete Steps 1, 2, and 3, but don't get the big payout, such as
  - *the employees and investors of Enron, Richard Nixon, lots of people whose names we'll never know.*
- Practically no one used to skip Step 3 and still wind up at Step 4 until they invented reality television, including
  - *the Kardashians and an increasing number of "real" housewives.*

For the other 99.5 percent of us, the cracks in this model have been there long before anyone coined the terms *millennial* or *GenZ*. Without delving too much into the changing nature of capital, shifting socioeconomic trends, or the demise of face-to-face contact, suffice it to say that success early in life does not always indicate success in later life.

Which is what makes life exciting for we non-Freds.

- Just because someone gets into a great school doesn't mean that they are going to land a plum job.
- Just because someone lands a plum job doesn't mean that they have already landed on easy street.
- Just because someone works extremely hard at their job (and this truth is kind of sad in my opinion; I like to think of these people as all having the consolation of being a size 00 and whatever the male equivalent is of that) doesn't mean that they are going to be satisfied with how high they rise.
- Just because you're not on a traditional path to Step 4 doesn't mean that you can't still get there.

JerseyCoachAmy: *No, of course Freds are not the only model for happiness. Take another one of my cousins, whom I will call Weller. (Weller happens to be his real name too. Valentine and Leopoldina are real family names as well, but I digress . . .) Weller is not motivated by money or the spotlight; he has more than he needs of the former and actively avoids the latter. Weller is motivated, like so many people I have had the pleasure of working with through the years, by the luxury of doing what he loves to do every day. Because for all his career, Weller has worked in the professional sports world and been intimately involved with his favorite sport at the highest level. He has circled the world dozens of times, something of which a kid from New Jersey could only dream. Now, one of the other great loves of his life, his daughter,*

> *has carved her own path in his favorite sport as well. So no, Captain*
> *Critical, I don't think careers are all about chasing money and fame.*
> *Work can purely be a means to do what you love.*

What does this mean for you? Your whole career is ahead of you. It doesn't matter whether you move to Step 2 at age eighteen or age forty— you, too, can become a Fred. As it turned out, very few of the friends I envied for being so far ahead of me so fast in those first few years out of college became Freds. Or if they did, it was not on the route where they started. If you are feeling like the dog that has not yet had its day, just keeping working on finding what is right for you. Life can amaze you.

Summary

- Everyone has thought about what kind of jobs they might like to have someday. While the world may already be saturated with pop stars and iconic athletes, discovering/knowing what you like and don't like doing provides clues as to what may be realistic for you as a focus. Write down some thoughts about what you like and what you are good at doing. Step back and see what you learn about yourself.

- Jobs are made up of basic activities that you do in life—activities you probably do without thinking too much about them. Break down the activities you like doing into the skills they require. Yoga takes patience and concentration, while organizing a hockey league takes planning, and organizing, and making connections. When you break down what you like doing into the tasks and skills required, you'll begin to see how those tasks and skills can translate into jobs.

- You can identify what you're good at doing by starting with examples, then see how that can translate into a job skill. Rarely do people like doing things in which they are not competent. Do you opt to research the hotels and schedules when planning a trip or prefer to keep the budget spreadsheet? This one fact can tell you a lot about what you may enjoy doing professionally.

- Complete the simple exercise in this chapter to learn a lot more than you may have thought possible about yourself and your potential career interests. Be honest and take some time with it, but also know that you can always come back and refine or change your responses later.

- Don't fall into the trap of thinking that you must get your career trajectory right the first time. Lots of people don't get it right on the third, fourth, or even fifth time. And that's okay. Just remember that this happens to just about everyone, and that it is both totally normal and totally worth it to keep trying.

You hopefully know more now about yourself and how you can add value in a job. Our next step is to look at how to identify what kind of jobs may work for you. It's a great feeling to find one that you did not know existed, plays to all your strengths, fits your lifestyle, and pays you well. In the next chapter, let's go job hunting!

Chapter 3.
Link Your Objective to Job Categories

Now that you have an idea of what you may enjoy doing in a professional role, it's time to learn how to understand what types of jobs and organizations will find your contributions valuable. Happily, there are way more jobs out there than you could ever imagine and plenty of hiring managers that need your help meeting their goals.

Seriously! Sadly, finding the right jobs and hiring managers for you is not easy. Neither is it easy to understand exactly what you would do in these jobs, which is a key part of successful interviewing. You need to know how to do the research and link what you find to your own skills and objectives—which you soon will. In this chapter, we will learn

- why you, and most of the population, know so little about the kinds of jobs that are available;
- how to analyze a business to understand what kinds of jobs it offers; and
- how to talk to people in a way that will get them talking about their jobs.

This will help you further refine and narrow your job search objective, while at the same time, teach you soft networking skills that you will continue to build on as we move forward. Networking is a very valuable and misunderstood tool. Honestly, it is just talking to people about themselves—with a goal of asking to stay in touch in case they may be able to help with your job search. And there are two things that are true about everyone who is adulting: We like talking about ourselves, and we've all had to look for a job so we know how hard it can be.

In this chapter, you'll learn how to do what I call "soft networking," or how to get people to tell you what they do. Soft networking means you are simply gathering information, meeting people, and taking the "scary" out of discovering what do people actually do in jobs." Who knows? It might even be fun.

JerseyCoachAmy: *The careers you think are cool will evolve and change the more you learn. Many people start out wanting to be a superhero or a Ninja then their career choices change as the kinds of movies they watch change. The kinds of jobs that leading characters in movies have can be hard to get.* [1] *Here's the deal: there are way more jobs than those. Jobs that are interesting and rewarding. Jobs that will make you feel good about yourself. You just don't know about them. You need to get away from your computer and talk to people to find out about them. Am I saying that every day will be awesome in one of these yet-to-be-identified jobs? No. But you also may not end up at odds with the Fed, an evil sorceress, or a shadow-government plot on Christmas Eve. So, there's that.*

I grew up always knowing that my parents met at work and what they actually did. From offices in New York City's Pan Am building immediately after WWII, my father set up overseas airline offices to support the growing commercial airline industry. My mother shopped for the

---

[1] Doctor, lawyer, politician, rock star, drug kingpin, organized-crime boss, media personality, beloved country veterinarian, unsung artisan, corporate titan, regular guy or gal with a big secret, teacher with the biggest heart, super scientist, evil scientist, mad scientist, diplomat, spy, tech wizard, secret android, etc.

families of the employees he sent overseas to run offices; those families had little access to commercial goods while Europe was rebuilding. Cool, right? I thought so. (Did you suddenly think you are reading a book by Methuselah?[2] I am old, but in my defense, my parents were really old when they had me.) Because my parents' work got me interested in jobs, I developed a really annoying habit as a kid of asking people what they actually *did* in their jobs. Not because I wanted to know how much money they made but because I was curious to know what people did all day. I collected a lot of information, and even more questions. I also learned that most people don't generally want to talk about what they actually do when they are not actually doing it.

> **JerseyCoachAmy:** *People are not trying to be jerks when they either brush you off or start talking to you as if you obviously understand yield curve risk and how rising interest rates impact Treasury prices, and "Hey, maybe you would like to work in bond trading?" But because I know from lots of experience how people tend to respond to a general query about their jobs, I've added a section here about how to effectively ask people about their jobs/their work, and how to break down their answers into pieces that you can digest. Read it. Practice it. No one is going to spoon-feed you the information you need.*

Which generally leaves the bulk of jobs in the world a mystery to the average person. People often don't know what their closest friends or relatives actually do on a day-to-day basis, because asking can be awkward: For the person who is being asked (a.k.a. 'the Explainer'), it can seem overwhelming to present what happens daily to someone who is

---

[2] Methuselah is a figure in Judaism, Christianity, and Islam known for the longest human lifespan of all those given in the Bible, 969 years. In other words, known for being old. *Super, super old.*

not familiar with the industry; and for the person who is interested in learning (a.k.a. 'the Questioner'), asking questions can be intimidating.

For example, let's say you ask a friend's mom about her job. You know she is a scientist and works in healthcare. She will tell you she does early-stage drug research for a biopharmaceutical company. Her job is intimately tied to approving drug development ideas moving from Phase I of development to Phase II. For her to really explain her work, you would need to understand, at a minimum, how drugs hoping to gain FDA approval move through all the phases of the development cycle and what the key criteria are at each stage. She would need to talk to you about marketability, indications, contra-indications, and other terms that you may not know if you are not in the industry. So, it may be a little overwhelming for her to consider how to give you a strong understanding without first providing a primer on the industry, which is not what you asked for.

Explainers can become easily frustrated. Questioners always worry about sounding ignorant.

JerseyCoachAmy: *There really are no dumb questions. That is truly a thing. Get your own Jersey on and always ask—even when someone musters their most authoritative voice and throws around acronyms or big words. Ask what the acronyms mean. I guarantee you will not be the only one in the room who has no clue what the person is talking about, even though everyone else is smiling and nodding.*

This chapter will focus on getting you thinking about what jobs there are in the world beyond the ones you already know of or interact with or see on television. Then we'll talk about how to ask effective questions about other peoples' jobs that will get them talking in a way that will give you practical help. Every job you learn about gets you closer to identifying the job you do (and don't) want.

Why You Don't Know What Jobs Exist

Most people only talk about work with their coworkers or others in their industry. The reason is that every organization has its own short-hand, acronyms, goals, and pressures that create barriers for individuals to talk about their work with those who don't work in the organization or are not involved in the industry.

If you were to ask, "What do you do for work?" you'll most likely get a sound bite that doesn't really tell you anything. Furthermore, when pressed, most people have trouble explaining "the forest" and so only detail out "the trees," so it's not terribly informative. Take this example:

RYAN: "So, what do you do for work?"

ALICIA: "I'm in sales at a software firm that provides data security services."

This is where "normal" people often end the conversation. However, if Ryan were going to do a little job sleuthing, he could continue by asking:

RYAN: "So, what does that mean you do? Give a lot of presentations to potential customers?"

ALICIA: "No, actually I'm in Customer Success, so I only work with customers after they have bought the product. I take their complaints and compliments. I ask about additional features that may be valuable, then work with our developers to try to build those features. Similarly, if there is a bug or problem with the product, I will work with internal teams to make sure the bug gets fixed."

So, will poor Ryan ever going to ask anyone again what they do after making the mistake of thinking that Alicia is a salesperson because she is in sales? Hopefully Alicia will be nice and explain this to him:

RYAN: "Well, I feel stupid."

ALICIA: "Don't. Think about it this way: acquiring a new customer is expensive. As an analogy, think about having to rent an apartment. You have to put up first month's rent, last month's rent, a deposit, and sometimes pay a broker's fee. It's expensive. To make that apartment worth all that upfront cost, you are going to want to stay a while.

Then think about all the costs associated with getting a new customer: meals, travel, a portion of marketing and sales salaries, demos, training. It's expensive. To make all that upfront investment worth it, you are going to want to make that customer, and the revenue they bring you, stay a while. That is where Customer Success comes in. Once the sale of a product or service is complete, the Customer Success team makes sure that you are happy with the solution you received so that you will continue your relationship with the company—because the company spent a lot of money to get you in the door."

Now it makes sense, right? And not such a dumb question after all.

After I finally became a bank trainee back in the dark ages, part of the program was to rotate through all of the major areas of the bank to understand how things worked on a grassroots level. We rotated through all the departments to gain an understanding of what they did and how they interacted with each other. Often, I would sit at someone's desk, and they would carefully explain that a form or file would arrive in their inbox, they would review the document for certain information, perhaps add additional information, check the document against computer records, and then put the document in their outbox.

"Where did the document come from?" I would ask.

"Where does the document go?" I would ask.

Sometimes I got answers, and sometimes I got blank stares. It's a strange phenomenon for people to only see their piece of the puzzle, but it's not uncommon. The good news is that a little common sense goes a long way towards understanding, once you've got the hang of analyzing jobs and businesses.

Let me give you an example of what I mean. In the next section, we'll take a common business and break it down into the widely varied set of jobs and skills that it requires to run profitably. You can apply this kind of analysis to any service or product, and when you do, you'll start to realize there is huge variety of jobs in the world—many of which can fit your interests, skills, and objectives.

About the Many, Many, Many Kinds of Jobs There Are

Almost all my clients are shocked when they realize how many kinds of jobs there are, and how many are hiding in plain sight. The goods and services you use every day have been built on a huge number of interesting and valuable jobs. Even when you do something very simple like buy a cup of coffee from your favorite independent hip spot, you are experiencing the result of an incredibly diverse set of skills and careers. Let's look at how many jobs bring you your coffee every morning.

Setting aside the obvious roles of barista, cashier, and cleaning staff, think about the

- commercial real estate agent that leases that space for the owner of the building;
- logo or branding company that was hired to create a recognizable image and name;
- decorator, architect, and contractor that designed the space to match what the store wanted for its hip vibe, and sourced all the furniture and lighting and art;

- signage company that developed both the exterior and interior signage;
- manager who needs to get all required health code, safety, and fire permits, schedule employee shifts, interview, hire and train new employees when there is turnover, and make sure all runs smoothly;
- buyer who sources the ingredients for the coffee and the food;
- chef who develops an accompanying menu, and identifies how the menu can be reproduced quickly and reliably;
- buyer who contracts for paper products with the salesperson for the paper company, and who then works with them to make sure the shop is well-stocked and properly invoiced for the paper goods used in the kitchen, bathrooms, and at the counter;
- accountant who keeps track of how much revenue the store is bringing in, how much the store is spending, and how much is netted in profit;
- executive who decides what to do with the profit (if there is any).

And many more (building inspector, cleaning product supplier, website creator, marketing rep, health inspector—to name a few others). Imagine how much more complicated this gets if this one store becomes three, or six, or ten.

JerseyCoachAmy: *Don't just go into a store and buy stuff anymore. Likewise, don't just go online and order stuff. Instead, think about the work that it takes to present and deliver that item to you: manufacturing, pricing, selection, packaging, content development, signage, etc. There are a lot of freakin' jobs associated with getting a new pair of socks.*

Think about buying your coffee from a chain the size of Starbucks. You can be sure:

- People have gone all over the world to source your beans and negotiate with local growers, governments, and transportation agencies to bring those beans to a processor. (Starbucks also purchases plantations and then runs them in different parts of the world. Think about running an organization of that size on top of their retail behemoth!)
- Huge teams of data scientists work on algorithms to best sort out/ improve the logistics of getting the processed beans to the vast network of stores using multiple forms of transportation for processing, as well as shipping the beans while they're fresh across continents, and creating different blends for that "just right" test.
- Algorithms get written and tweaked regularly for getting the right number of cups to each store each day. After all, you can't sell coffee without cups, but each location has a limited amount of storage space.
- Departments monitor the inventory and cash-flow levels of thousands of accessory products—such as mugs, home-brewing equipment, and bagged coffee—to identify whether an item is selling so well it needs to be reordered, or whether revenue is sluggish and the item needs to be discounted, or maybe discontinued.
- Real estate teams are looking at the saturation rates for market share on both large- and small-scale markets all over the world and analyzing, both quantitatively and qualitatively, the potential impact that future store investments can have on the stock price.

Just to name a few. It's an amazing collection of tasks, and every one of them makes common sense when you understand them. Once you start to see the job market from this perspective, you'll start to realize the significant depth and breadth of the potentially available roles there are for you in the job market.

The easiest way to start learning about jobs that may appeal to you is by starting to talk to people. Talk to lots of people: your college career office, friends that have graduated, your friends' parents and your parents' friends. Ask neighbors. Ask your old camp counselors. Ask people you meet in line for (you guessed it) coffee who seem interesting.

But didn't I just say that people don't really like to talk about what they do? I did.

Here's the thing: everyone has been where you are now. Either they wish they'd had someone who could have helped them when they were starting out, or they were lucky enough to have someone who did help them, and they know how meaningful it is. Almost everyone you ask will spend time with you if they can. What you need to do is make it easy for *them* to make it meaningful for *you*.

What to Say to People So They Will Talk about Their Jobs

You already took the first step in Chapter 2 by identifying your area of interest: what you may be interested in doing (your objective), why you feel you can add value (your skills), and what you would enjoy doing (your interests). That is the information you need to present. The next thing you want to do is get the person in front of you talking in a way that helps you understand whether or not they're in a career you'd be interested in pursuing.

Here's the way a typical exchange may go:

Question:	Answers:		
"What do you do for work?"	"I'm in advertising."	"I'm in the regulatory department of a company that sells software to doctors."	"I work in operations at a retail store."

You can ask a follow-up to your initial question: "So, I'm starting a job search and trying to learn what people *actually do* in their work. What does that *actually* mean you spend your time doing?" The answers you get will likely be something like:

	Advertising Example	Software Example	Retail Example
"What does that actually mean?"	"I work for an advertising agency in their database department, mostly tracking the number of responses we get to an ad across multiple delivery platforms to see which has the highest performance."	"I follow all legislation and regulation issues associated with health insurance at the state level. I summarize the issues monthly to keep our developers knowledgeable about how changes may impact our software."	"I handle requests for replacement fixtures due to theft and damages at Old Navy."

These answers tell you more, but they start in the middle of the story, not at the beginning. And they still don't necessarily give you what you need to evaluate whether they may be jobs that you would like to do.

However, there are questions you can ask about what people actually do in their jobs that can get them to go back to the basics. The following questions are universal to all jobs, so you never have to be concerned about asking one that does not apply:

- "What does the company do? How does it make money?"
- "Who is the customer that actually buys the product/service, and why?"

- "What companies does your company compete against, and how?"
- "What does your team or department do to support the company overall?"
- "How do you help your team or department?"

We'll talk more about these questions in later chapters, too, because they play a role in prepping for an interview: if you can answer them it will show that you understand the environment and role for which you are applying. In this context/moment, however, you're just gathering data— maybe to keep in a notebook and maybe just to keep in your head—to see if this person does a job that might fit the objective you selected for yourself in Chapter 1.

By asking the right questions you can learn some really valuable things about how companies and industries work, and generally, people will be flattered in your interest. The answers you get will be in real time: real-world learning that can expand your knowledge and your network. Talking about work outside of work may not be high on everyone's list but having someone take an interest in what they do can be nice. From your perspective, you only need to spend a few minutes and ask some targeted questions to figure out how other people spend their time at work.

Four targeted questions about a company can give you a really good overview, and (as outlined in the table below) give you very different and detailed answers:

- How does a company make money?
- What is it that a client or customer is actually buying, and why?
- How does the company compete against similar products/services offered?
- How does the job they do support how the company makes money?

To help you structure and record your conversations as well as do the additional prep outlined below, you will find a worksheet for this exercise in the accompanying workbook, also available from on my site, www.jobcoachamy.com/downloads.

	Marketing Example	Software Example	Retail Example
"What does the company do? How does it make money?"	"It helps retailers identify how to get the 'biggest bang' for their advertising dollar by testing campaigns on various websites to see how well they do."	"It builds a software package that doctors can use to schedule follow-up appointments and lab tests, order prescriptions, see patient records, and send bills to insurance companies—all from one handheld device."	"It sells affordable casual clothing and work-out gear to men, women, and children—both online and in retail stores."
"Who is the customer that actually buys the product/ service, and why?"	"Any company that uses online ads could use us, but we specialize in retailers like Zappos and Macy's. We can also be sub-contracted by agencies that only do creative but not testing."	"Doctors' offices purchase a monthly subscription. They can also purchase additional modules for billing and record-keeping."	"Men, women, and children— for themselves or their families."

	Marketing Example	Software Example	Retail Example
"What companies does the company you work for compete against, and how?"	"Lots of other companies are in this space: Some only do campaign testing, some put together all the creative and then do the testing (i.e., 'fully integrated'), while others do stand-alone testing, like we do. Also, some companies test on their own with software they can license."	"Doctors who are not willing to switch to software to do these traditional tasks. Other software packages purchased by hospital systems, not individual doctors' offices, that do not interface with our systems."	"All other casual clothing companies, usually on price."

	Marketing Example	Software Example	Retail Example
"What does your team or department do to support the company overall?"	"I place the ads and analyze the 'click through' data to see how many consumers actually clicked on the ad, how many went to the site, and how many purchased something as a result of the ad. I use statistics programs to compare results. So if, for example, a dog food company places two different ads on the same site, I evaluate which one resulted in more sales."	"What insurance will and will not cover can change quickly, and we need to update our software as quickly as those changes are made or our doctor customers get frustrated. My team keeps the developers updated on changes they need to make so the doctors are using updated software. That way, a doctor will not [mistakenly] tell a patient that insurance will pay for a procedure that is actually no longer being covered."	"I work in a region with 100 stores. To keep our costs down, the stores don't have much in the way of 'décor.' But we do have our famous mannequins, and of course we have to have lighting. When there are issues with lighting or mannequins, people call my team to get them replaced. We are considered part of marketing because at our organization the budget for decorating the stores is considered [to be part of] marketing."

	Marketing Example	Software Example	Retail Example
"How do you help your team or department?"	"My results are placed in a presentation with some other results, and they help the client to make a decision about where to spend their advertising budget."	"I keep a calendar of pending legislation in three states. Then I work with the developers to make sure that if a change is coming as a result of that/a vote, they understand the impact as to what change it will have and when."	"I actually call the factory that makes our mannequins and order new arms or legs or dog heads, and have them shipped to the store that requested them. I also bill the store directly and make sure the missing piece arrives on time. Each year, I estimate how many heads, limbs, and torsos we will need for the region and negotiate the best pricing and delivery to meet our needs."

> **JerseyCoachAmy:** *You can't just start asking people about what they do for a living and expect to good information. Think about how much you enjoy people asking you what you enjoy about school, and what you are studying in your classes. How well does that usually go?*

Who do you plan to approach to get information on what they do?	When will you ask them if they're willing to meet with you to talk briefly about their work?	Write down how you will start the conversation: Why you are asking for their time and what you hope to get out of the conversation.	Write down how you will close the conversation, and if you will ask for follow-up.
Example: Your friend's mom who is a buyer for a big department store.	*At the neighborhood holiday party over winter break.*	*I'm starting to think about what I want to do after graduation and was wondering if I could ask you about what you actually do at your job.*	*Thank you so much. I am going to do a little more research. May I follow up with you by email in the months ahead as I continue to pursue this?*

A couple of important tips:

- Explain that you are just trying to do research about what you want to do and to figure out what jobs there are; most people have been where you are now so will be empathetic.
- Use your best judgment if you feel someone is getting annoyed,

and if so, back off. Sometimes you are just not going to get a straight answer.

- Keep a notebook or digital file to record what you've learned so that you can refer to it. Ask permission to write it down while you are chatting, or write things down immediately afterwards.
- Use the universal questions I've provided above as a jumping-off point; the best questions to ask are the ones to which you want to know the answers.
- Never be shy about being curious: interest-*ed* is interest-*ing*.

If someone offers to help you, take their contact information and be sure to thank them. However, at this stage, unless you are really set on fire by what you have learned, you should let them know you are just doing research and not ready to start a conversation about anything more than that yet. Circle back with them, however, to thank them for being interested in helping you.

> **JerseyCoachAmy:** *Watch someone's eyes when you ask about how they got started on their career. You'll likely see sheer panic first as the memories of those days hit them in the face like a bucket of cold water. Then, hopefully, you'll see empathy blossom, and that's when you know you've got them on the hook to help you.*

In the next chapter, we'll talk about whom to approach with this new skill and how. Asking people questions is just one part of an overall research plan to identify specifically what may be out there for you.

Summary

- Of course, you can't know exactly what you may want to do! How could you know what jobs are out there? People don't really talk about what they do because their work may be hard to understand out of context, or it's not fun for them to try and explain it.

- Once you start to think about how basic products and services are delivered, you can start to see how a lot of different kinds of jobs are required. Just the shop that gives you coffee has people working in it who love: foreign travel, doing interior design, building algorithms, cooking, sales, and countless more kinds of jobs. If you think about it that way, jobs are like apps: if there is something that is of interest to you, more than likely "there's an job for that."

- So how do you take your focus and start learning about what jobs may be out there for you? People do want to help you. Almost everyone has been where you are. However, they are not used to talking about their jobs, and the world of work is not always easy to understand or explain. Asking people a few basic questions about their industry and company will help both of you set a framework for a meaningful discussion.

- Interest-*ed* is interest-*ing*. People like to talk about themselves. To break the ice, ask them how they wound up in their job or how they got started in their careers, then start asking more specific questions. The more people you get to talk about themselves, the more fascinating a conversationalist you become.

Chapter 4.
Do Some Research

You have now accomplished two milestones! You have a sense of how your skill set and interests may translate into the professional world, and you understand how to approach people to learn more about what jobs may be available and of interest to you.

Now it's time for a plan! The planning process is likely one that you will do more than once in your lifetime. This process also makes sense to do annually, or every other year, to learn about new trends in businesses and careers. There is never a shortage of content on either subject, so coming back to this planning process regularly can be both valuable and fascinating. The process can also protect you from the risk that everyone faces as they grow in their careers: becoming boring and increasingly able to speak knowledgeably about only one area. Again, and I can't say it often enough, interest-*ed* is interest-*ing*.

Talking to people, reading job descriptions, and setting simple goals for yourself during this phase of the process are the three concrete steps you will need to take to get started. (Remember—I warned you about threes?) In this chapter we'll cover:

- How to start soft networking
- Reading job descriptions
- Setting simple goals

Doing these three things will help you get a much greater sense of what might be available to you from your network and in the market when you begin the formal search process. You will also start yourself on the path to becoming disciplined about your job search by spending a set amount of time each week for this work and recording your progress in a central location. You'll want to keep track of all your activities during this period, either digitally or by hand, and you'll also want to set aside a date for this research period to end and for the actual job search process to begin.

In the chapters ahead, we'll pull everything together in a more formal manner and link the tools and an actual timeline to this process. But right now, we are still learning to gather information.

Start Soft Networking

We've talked about how to talk to people *effectively* about jobs and careers, but how can you talk to people *comfortably*? Talking to people about jobs and careers is outside of most people's comfort zones. However, it's really the best way to learn about what's out there and, more importantly, what may be out there for *you*.

The first thing I recommend doing is read Dale Carnegie's *How to Win Friends and Influence People*.[1] Although written more than eighty years ago, the book is still considered one of the best business books of all time. When you read the book, you will learn that asking people to talk about themselves is a shortcut to becoming the most well-liked person in any room. Armed with what you learn from Mr. Carnegie and what you learned in the last chapter, talking to people about jobs and careers will seem a lot less intimidating.

Next, you'll want to think about *whom* you need to get talking. My advice is to start anywhere. You can gather information relevant to

---

[1] Originally published in 1936 by Simon & Schuster, Carnegie's *How to Win Friends and Influence People* has been revised and republished many times and is widely available in many formats. Visit its Wikipedia page to learn about the book's interesting history.

your skills and interests from family, friends, neighbors, alumni of any school you ever attended, your hairstylist, people in line with you at the grocery store; or anyone you sit next to on a plane, or meet walking your dog, or at your latte spot, or at a meetup, or in a Twitter chat, or at church. Seriously, I know people who have gotten great information, contacts, and even jobs through each of these channels. It could happen to you.

Your neighbor who is never home on weekends may have one of those jobs that is of interest to you in retail management, but you would see firsthand that success would mean working almost every weekend.

Your hairstylist may tell you about a client who is starting their own firm in digital design but then whisper that due to moving from retail management to digital design, this aspiring entrepreneur can only afford to come in once a year.

A group of nonprofit project managers on a twitter chat may be really encouraging to you that theirs is a great job and career route, but they may also warn you to stay away from a few particular organizations because they are managed poorly.

There is information to be had almost everywhere, so start where you are comfortable talking to people, write things down, don't pass along gossip, and see what you learn.

In Chapter 7, we'll talk about networking in a more focused way and learn how to get people thinking about their own network and how they may be able to offer real help. At this point, however, you are just gathering as much information as you can to inspire your own research.

> **JerseyCoachAmy:** *Start learning what kind of life you want as you start learning what kind of job you want. But don't limit yourself to stereotypes. You can choose a job in finance, healthcare, retail, software, tech, or clean energy that requires a forty-hour week or an eighty-hour week. It depends on the company and its culture, the*

> *actual role you are doing, and how well you can do it. There are*
> *limitless possibilities at this stage. Don't make assumptions.*

Conversations where you can gather information begin in one of two ways: (1) where someone asks what you are considering for your next move, or (2) when you initiate and ask what someone else does or how they got started. Here are some suggested ways to handle each situation.

When someone asks how your job search is going:

- Your instinct at this point may be to avoid the subject. However, take the counterintuitive route and ask for ideas, opinions, and facts. You never know what may come of them! Your questioner will most likely be flattered that his or her opinion is of interest to you.
    - "I'm just getting started. What is the best advice you ever got?"
- Be open about the work you have done so far on your interests, even if it is vague:
    - "I know I'm not going to be good behind a desk."
    - "I'm going to be looking for something where I can work in a lab."
    - "I like the idea of doing something in a start-up environment where there is a team and goal, and where I can commit to working really hard for the success of both."
- Be honest. If you don't know or haven't thought enough yet, that's okay. It's perfectly acceptable to say:
    - "I need to think about what I've liked doing in my life so far and what I've been good at doing. I'm not sure yet how that will translate into something that I will be good at and enjoy doing in a work environment. Once I've got that figured out, may I contact you?"

When you are asking for information as part of your job search research:

- Lead with something that makes no assumptions but indicates why you are asking. For example, "I'm trying to learn all I can about what people do as I approach a transition. Do you have a career you enjoy?"
- If you are approaching someone who works in a city or region where you would like to be, don't hesitate to ask for advice about how to make the transition there. You might say, "Do you have any advice for someone who is seeking to make a life for themselves in Seattle?"
- Similarly, if you know someone to be in a profession of interest, use the same technique. Ask them, "Do you have any advice for someone who is seeking to get into the brokerage business?"
- When asking someone about careers outside of their area of expertise, lead with your own interests but acknowledge theirs. You can venture, "I understand you are a programmer at a major computer software firm. I am interested in learning more about careers in sales. Would you mind telling me what sales is like at your firm?"

For both:

- Don't be surprised if people just want to be polite and are happy to/want to leave after one exchange. If somebody is willing to engage and talk to you about their own journey, listen for as long as they will talk! Be sure to get their email and thank them. The exchange will mean something to both of you.

The next element of your research plan can be equally informative and productive at this point, *and* you can do the next step from the comfort of your home day or night: simply go online and read job descriptions. The Internet is happy to help.

Read Job Descriptions

Job descriptions provide an excellent education on what is available in the market for a particular skillset within a particular market area. They are generally structured in four parts:

1. An overall description of the company, with some editorial thrown in about its success and what a great place it is to work. You can go to the company's website to get a better idea of what happens there, see who their customers are, and maybe even read a case study on a piece of business it recently performed. If you're really interested, search the Internet for the company's competitors and products. Maybe the industry has its own association(s) that can provide more information about careers in the business you're looking at and the industry as a whole.

2. An outline of the job itself, including what duties will need to be performed, what the performance expectations will be, whether there will be travel involved, and other highly relevant details. More specs will likely be provided at the interview stage.

3. A list of requirements necessary to be considered for the job. If some skills or years of experience, for example, are "nice to have" but not necessary, they will be noted as such, (e.g., "Knowledge of spoken Mandarin a plus"). Pay close attention to what is a requirement for the job versus what would be attractive. If there are "must have" skills, these will also be noted (e.g., "Must have three years of prior experience in managing technical projects."). Take these "must haves" seriously, but don't blow them out of proportion. In other words, you can likely get this job without knowing Mandarin, but if you only have two years of experience managing technical projects, go ahead and apply!

Many of my clients tend to write off a role if they don't check every box, but I think this is a mistake.

4. The last section may mention competitive salary and benefits, or legalese such as you needing to be able to lift ten pounds or sit for long periods of time. If there are no deal breakers for you in this language, you should not be put off from applying.

We'll talk a lot more about analyzing job descriptions, but for now, just read them to see which ones seem interesting.

Research indicates that men and women react to job descriptions differently.[2] Studies show that when a man possesses three out of ten job qualifications, his reaction is more likely to be, "I can do this job! I'm going for it!" The same studies indicate that a woman who possesses eight out of ten requirements of a job description will more likely react with, "I can't do this job if I don't have all ten. It is probably not worth the time to apply."

While it is not my field of expertise by any measure, I can tell you that recruiting is a major leverage point for achieving the goal of gender parity in the workplace. There has been a significant amount of research done to date that is easily accessible through a basic Google search ("recruiting, gender bias") if you would like to know more. Below is a very high-level summary for the generally curious.

- The fact is that gender discrimination does exist in job descriptions.[3]

---

[2] Tara Sophia Mohr, "Why Women Don't Apply for Jobs Unless They're 100% Qualified," *Harvard Business Review*, August 25, 2014, https://hbr.org/2014/08/why-women-dont-apply-for-jobs-unless-theyre-100-qualified.

[3] https://www.sussex.ac.uk/webteam/gateway/file.php?name=gendered-wording-in-job-adverts.pdf&site=7.

- This was discovered because, completely unconsciously, certain descriptive words that find their way into job descriptions tend to be viewed as either masculine (e.g., decisive) or feminine (e.g., cooperative).
- Gender-influenced wording only impacts women and has no impact on men.
- Software tools have become available for companies to screen their job descriptions for gender bias; they can also implement gender-diverse panels to audit their job descriptions.

The bottom line is: apply for the job, even if you don't think you're qualified. What's the worst that can happen?

Sign up for two to four job alerts on a major job search board. I find LinkedIn and Indeed best for corporate postings. Idealist is best for mission-driven organizations and volunteer roles. Many industries have their own specialized job boards such as Doccupations.com for the dental community and Lawcrossing.com for the legal community. Sign up using keywords suggested below or, preferably, based on your own interests. Some geographic boards are good, such as WorkNOLA in New Orleans, LA. You will receive no shortage of job descriptions to read. You may need to refine your key words until you find one or two alerts that are relevant. Just putting key words and location into Google will give you what's available on *every* board. This can be overwhelming or time-saving, depending on your point of view.

Public-sector work can be found primarily the same way. Occasionally there are local, state, and federal postings on the sites mentioned above. I find GovernmentJobs.com is the most comprehensive resource for city, state, federal and public sector jobs. USAjobs.com has federal-only jobs, every state will have its own state employment site, etc. Jobs can range from basic labor to administration to specialized roles like engineering and training. You can also work for the public sector through a private company that contracts with the government, such as Ernst & Young or Verizon.

If you have some "goal companies," go directly to their sites to receive new listings. With alerts, expect to receive a lot more postings than you can read every morning but make a commitment to read a minimum number each day.

JerseyCoachAmy: *Be wary of company descriptions that use beautiful words to describe the company's mission and goals but don't mean anything useful. You may find that a company describing itself as an environmentally committed organization providing the best in logistical transportation support to global companies is, in fact, a box company. Make sure you know what the company does, even as you prepare to parrot their words back to them.*

With each new job description you read, there is the opportunity to learn

- what jobs there are that can leverage your skills;
- what companies are hiring;
- what roles may be worth an application, and what roles may be ones to aspire to;
- what does and does not interest you;
- what locations are hiring;
- the kinds of benefits, travel, and environments that are involved in certain jobs;
- what skills you might want to acquire (for example if SQL,

accounting, or SalesForce start showing up in the required or "nice to have" sections of a lot of job descriptions you like, you can start looking for free introductory skills courses online in these areas);

- that a skill or course you already have under your belt is showing up a lot for certain job descriptions; and

- in all likelihood, a few other things—like patterns and trends for certain roles, industries, or cities.

Sample Search Terms

(Try a few of these until you get one that seems to return the most relevant jobs for you. Results WILL vary.)

Industry	Function	Career Stage	Skill
Retail	Human Resources	Entry Level	Spanish Fluency
Financial Services	Informational Technology	Manager	SAP
Health Care	Marketing	Director	Ruby
Clean Energy	Logistics	Vice President	Salesforce
Technology	Customer Relationship	Senior Manager, C-Suite	Quantitative Analysis

Note: Be wary of sponsored ads in your search results or on job boards. These may be placed by third-party recruiters (see the accompany workbook for more information about third-party recruiters) or the jobs and companies may not be exactly as advertised. You want to make sure there is a salary, a clear description of tasks, and a company with a public website before you go anywhere for an interview or agree to work for a trial period of time.

Keep track of what you learn in the job descriptions that are important to you. For example, if you started out with the key works "entry level" and "online retail," this is what you may have learned after reading twenty to thirty job descriptions:

- A key role is "category management," which is managing a group of like products such as towels or lamps.
- Entry-level jobs involve a lot of quantitative skills like pricing and spreadsheet work as well as good written and verbal skills/communication.
- You get to work with designers and photographers in staging the products.
- There seem to be a lot of jobs at entry level supporting category managers, and the people in director-level jobs manage a group of categories.

Another good idea, especially if you are wondering what the long-term implications are for a certain path, is to search for senior roles in a function and/or field in which you may be interested so you have an idea of what you would be doing if you stayed on that career path or in a particular company. If you wanted to identify what kind of role you could have in a few years in the high-tech sales field, for example, you could look for "sales," "director level," and "software."

Here is an example summary of what you may have learned from that search:

- Director-level sales roles require five to seven years of experience managing goals of more than $1 million but do not necessarily require experience with managing a team of direct reports.
- The fastest growing markets seem to be security, virtual reality, health care, and quantitative analytical software used for marketing. Specific industry background is not generally required.

- Jobs are either in major accounts or inside sales; major account sales require greater than 50 percent travel but look like they offer a more competitive salary base.

Job descriptions will also be important when we cover more intensive networking and interviewing in chapters 7 and 11. They can hold the key to unlocking a lot of the information you will need to prepare yourself well in both areas.

Talking to people and doing online research are great preliminary research tools to add to the self-analysis you are doing to identify where and how you can add value. The last piece to add in at this point is to set some simple goals for yourself.

JerseyCoachAmy: *Another weird thing that you will find when reading job descriptions, in addition to finding a lot of hyperbole that doesn't actually describe the job, is that the same job title can have a lot of different meanings. You can probably figure out pretty easily that a project manager at a construction company has a very different job than a project manager at a video-gaming company. However, be aware that there are more subtle distinctions.*

The "business development" function, for example, can be used to cover a lot of different activities. At some software companies, you may need to be an engineer to be in business development so that you can talk to other engineers (potential customers). However, another software company selling the same kind of product to the same kind of customer may call the process of combing through websites to identify decision makers at target companies (potential clients) a business development role. Same title, different skill sets. Stuff in the business world, like the regular world, only mostly makes sense.

Set Simple Goals

Identify when you want to start and end this research phase of your job search. Here are a couple of ideas:

- Set specific dates.
- If you're not under time pressure, let yourself do research for a long time, but set a date when this time period will end. While it's easy to tell yourself you are doing something when you are asking questions and reading job descriptions—really, this is just a preparation stage.
- If you're in college, the sooner you get started, the less anxious you will feel about the big changes you are facing or will face soon.

When your research phase ends, be sure to have a plan:

- Continue to ask questions and read the new job alerts that come in while you are getting your tools ready (Chapters 5–8) and networking. Your efforts will dovetail into each other, and you will see the benefits of that.

Sample Goal for Getting Started		
October 1–October 31	Ask three people per week to explain to me what they actually do.	Read ten job descriptions per week.

- Write down and review what you've learned.
  - Is there a particular industry or role that you think you would enjoy?
  - Do you have a good sense of what you are qualified to do?

- Do you know which companies are hiring in your area of interest?

The purpose of setting up some simple goals is to: (1) put a time limit on this phase so that you know that you are going to move on to developing your tools at some point, (2) protect you from having that "black hole" feeling where you know you should be doing something but are paralyzed from doing anything, and (3) provide you with an answer to anyone who asks, "What are you doing to prepare for that upcoming transition?"

> **JerseyCoachAmy:** *Seriously, if you want to get rid of that pit in your stomach every time you think about this or whenever someone else talks about an interview, do just one of these things. It's not rocket science and it doesn't take a lot of time. Get your head out of the sand. You can thank me later.*

You'll find a worksheet for a research plan in the accompanying or downloadable workbook (www.jobcoachamy.com/shop).

If, for whatever reason, you are not ready to start submitting applications, you can still do important work learning and researching. If you needed to be ready yesterday, don't skip this step! Instead, do research at the same time you are developing your tools—the next step in the process. The knowledge you acquire will make this step easier and the results more effective.

Summary

- The best way to start doing basic research on a potential career is to start talking to people. Collecting information from human beings about what you could be doing in certain roles, what kind of lifestyles they would afford, and whether you could see yourself doing them is the best way to begin to figure things out.

At first, you will feel out of your comfort zone. Some of the people you talk to may feel out of their comfort zone as well. Don't give up. Keep asking questions. Find the communication style that works best for you. Write things down. Revisit what you learn and corroborate it by asking more people. You are starting to learn to network, which is just a fancy way of saying that you are learning to talk to people who you maybe don't know well. You will start to get great benefits, rewarding experiences, and probably even gain some new friends along the way. Start practicing. A lot.

- Reading job descriptions is another good way to move up the steep learning curve of job searching and career research. Tools exist to bring more available job postings to your inbox every morning than you can possibly read. Over time, you will begin to learn which are relevant. You will add new job alerts to your search engines and eliminate others. You'll start to see buzzwords and phrases that you can research further to see if they are meaningful or just hyperbole (there is plenty of hyperbole in company and role descriptions). You'll get an education in who's hiring, what they are looking for, and how you would match up to the ideal candidate they are seeking. Job descriptions are a wealth of information and education at this stage—cast a wide net for reading. Make notes about skills you see repeatedly coming up under the jobs you want. Think hard about ways you may have developed those skills in some area of your life or can get experience in them through a free online course or volunteer role.
- Set simple goals for yourself at this stage to make sure that each week or each month you set aside some time to both talk to people and read job descriptions. Don't spend a lot of time during the weeks and months where you have a lot of conflicting

priorities. Vary your weekly commitment based on what else is going on in your life. Use your research plan to move you forward in your search. Setting weekly goals will allow you to accomplish something at the end of every week, even if you have not yet met your end goal of becoming employed.

PART II
Develop Tools

Chapter 5.
Develop a High-Impact Résumé

There is *a lot* of information out there about résumés: in books, blogs, podcasts, and from gosh darn certified experts. Some of what people would have you believe you need to know or do is opinion, not fact. My perspective is that there is not an absolutely 100 percent formulaically correct way to prepare a résumé. You only need to prepare your résumé in a way that catches the attention of the people whose attention you need catching—in a good way, not in a "Hey, look how awful this résumé is! Let's put this thing on the bulletin board in the hall for laughs, eh?" kind of way.[1]

In this chapter, we'll review the generally important things to know about developing a high-impact résumé (i.e., a résumé with a higher chance of getting you noticed), then look at specific guidelines for getting your résumé the right kind of attention. Then, I will show you some practical examples of "low-impact" turned "high-impact" résumés. Of course, your résumé is not the only tool you will need. It is a jumping-off point. The goal is to make you stand out from the sea of other candidates, and while there are no guarantees, there are best practices. Learning how to create a high-impact résumé is one of them. From there,

---

[1] I can say with virtual certitude that you should not lay awake at night worrying about this happening to your résumé. Never, ever, in my life have I seen this happen nor could I imagine it happening. Everyone has been in your shoes. *Everyone.*

we'll talk about the importance of making sure your LinkedIn profile matches your résumé and adds additional dimensions—LinkedIn is the *lingua franca* of digital networking, and your profile allows you to add to your story. Lastly, I'll give you some insight about how hiring managers and others can read between the lines of your résumé to form opinions about you in ways that may or may not be advantageous.[2]

The Generally Important Things to Know

The generally important things to know, as you approach developing and submitting your résumé, fall into eight categories.

1. Key Words Will Get You Past Ocular Readers and AI Systems.

It would be a safe bet to assume that your résumé will go through some kind of computer system before it even reaches an internal recruiter. Customize your résumé with key words from the job description so that you can get through a computerized screener as well as a human pair of eyes. For example, if the job requires knowledge of Python, a computer can eliminate all résumés that do not include the word "Python" on the submitted application.

Additionally, such screens look for anything that indicate you have specifically applied for *this* role at *this* firm. Customizing a few sentences in your cover letter about always having wanted to work in this industry and for this company because of its cutting-edge approach to *x*, or the amazing job the company has done for its clients with product *y*, can make all the difference for not only a human screener but also an algorithmic one.[3]

---

[2] Please don't stress too much about this. At some point, a lot of people, including me, experience periods of unemployment or underemployment. It is what it is.

3 https://www.npr.org/2012/10/06/162440531/why-companies-use-software-to-scan-resumes

2. You Have 7.4 Seconds.

Research indicates that once your résumé gets to a human reviewer, it will only get an average of 7.4 seconds of attention.[4] The document needs to make an immediate impact on the recruiter to get you into the short stack of candidates that will be seriously considered. You can achieve this by highlighting your strongest skills and experience and leaving out what's less important. White space on the page is your friend. My methodology includes highlighting the strongest and/or most relevant accomplishments from your résumé in your cover letter (more on that in the next chapter) to double the chance of drawing the reader's attention to your most salable skills and experience.

> **JerseyCoachAmy:** *Seven freakin' seconds! You need to focus on what you've accomplished, not just what you were responsible for, because you want to stand out like a freakin' Avenger!*

3. Summarizing Your Story Will Give You an Advantage.

A quick glance at your résumé should tell someone your story. Make it as easy as possible for a recruiter or connection to match what you are looking for based on your interests and experience to what they may have to offer or may need. Because you only have 7.4 seconds, your résumé basically needs to have a tantrum to get noticed.

Some people consider a summary sentence or career objective at the top of the résumé crucial. Others consider this concept to be a

---

[4] Research done by The Ladders https://www.theladders.com/career-advice/you-only-get-6-seconds-of-fame-make-it-count in 2012 used a tool called "eye tracking" on a group of professional recruiters over ten weeks to "record and analyze where and how long someone focuses when digesting a piece of information or completing a task." It updated this study in 2018 and found the average time had risen from 6 to 7.4 seconds. https://www.prnewswire.com/news-releases/ladders-updates-popular-recruiter-eye-tracking-study-with-new-key-insights-on-how-job-seekers-can-improve-their-resumes-300744217.html

gasp-worthy *"Never!"* Given the option, my preference is to put your story in the form of a summary sentence or two at the top of your résumé, regardless of where you are in your career. Why make someone guess?

What is more important than whether you state your story in one to two sentences at the top of your résumé, is that you possess, and can show that you possess, the ability to state your story in one or two sentences. Put your story in your cover letter, in your email, in your opening gambit over the phone, or during the introductions on a teleconference. But by the time you have a résumé, you should have a very good summary of your story. We'll talk more about this in Chapter 7 when we talk about developing an elevator pitch.

Here are some good examples of a summary sentence or career objective:

- Hardworking, goal-oriented, new college graduate seeks to add value in an administrative role.
- Recent graduate with a consistent track record of achieving sales goals through hard work, persistence, and excellent relationship-building skills.
- Highly quantitative and analytical industrial engineer, with depth of experience in technical and creative software.
- Communications major with strong organizational and relationship skills seeks to add value in a mission-driven organization.

Making it as easy as possible for someone to understand what you are looking for, how you can add value, and what you have accomplished is a key part of successful job searching. The faster that other people—recruiters, hiring managers, people you want to add to your network—understand what it is that you want and what value you can add, the faster they will be on your side.

Having a cogent story is a consistent theme, is key to developing your elevator pitch, and is important for interviewing skills. We will return to it again and again.

4. Name Your Résumé File for <u>the Company's</u> Convenience, Not Yours.

Name the files you submit to a potential employer for *their* convenience, not yours:

<u>WRONG:</u>   Name_Date

<u>RIGHT:</u>   Name_Position_JobCode

If you submit the file with just your name and the date, it is not going to be easy to find. If I'm the hiring manager, I'm not going to remember your name *and* the position for which you are interviewing. Why? Because I've probably got more than one open requisition and have seen more than a half dozen candidates for each. I *am* going to remember the job title or code I'm hiring for, and I'm going to open those résumés for a refresher to make decisions. Make it easier for me by adding the name of the position for which you are interviewing and I'm going to like you better: you have the kind of common sense I need on my team. People have lost out on offers for stupider reasons. Make it hard for me, and I may not be able to find you again.

> **JerseyCoachAmy:** *It's not a good idea to assume that all hiring managers are extremely well-organized. Let's say I saw your résumé to be an associate in my department when you applied a few weeks ago— and it looked good. But I got distracted and didn't print it out or save it to my candidates' folder. Now I'm ready to start interviewing, but your résumé file is titled Driscoll_Spring and is somewhere in the depths of my desktop. I'm not going to remember your name or, as a result, how to find your file. So, I'm going to move on. That's sad for you. But it happens. Help me out a little.*

5. Someone May Check Your Digital Profile to See If Your Claim of Industry Interest is True.

If you say you are devoted to finding a role in commercial real estate, be sure to join Commercial Real Estate industry groups on LinkedIn, Facebook, and Twitter. Look for blogs and influencers in the area. If your résumé gets noticed, they may check your digital profile to see if you are sincere in your interest. You may also find unexpected benefits, like professional associations with free job boards or interesting seminars with reduced membership prices to welcome new professionals to the field.

Similarly, for every company where you apply, be sure to follow them digitally. They may check to make sure your interest in them is genuine. Remember how we talked about how the job always goes to the person who wants it the most? Maybe it comes down to you and one other person, and the other person follows the company. You never know.

6. Have Someone Else Review Before You Hit Send.

Be sure to have at least one other set of eyes on your résumé AND your cover letter to look for typos, grammatical errors, or anything that may be confusing. Use all the available tools on your word processor and/or apps like Grammarly. When you've been looking at a document for a long time, you can become blind to even the most glaring of typos. Reviewing a résumé and cover letter is easy for someone else to do and could save you from getting thrown out of the process before you have even begun.

7. You Need to Present Yourself as Someone Who Can Add Value.

Getting your résumé into the right hands to be seen and evaluated is a big part of the battle, but it's only the first step. Beyond your strategy and tactics for applying, you need to be able to present yourself as someone who is going to be worth the salary that has been budgeted for the position to which you are applying. What it all boils down to is how much value you will be able to add.

So, what does this mean for résumé content?

Don't think of your résumé as a tool for presenting how great *you are*, but as a tool for presenting how great *you would be to have on a team*. A hiring manager gets dozens to hundreds of candidates that present themselves as being "Grrrrrrreat!" Of those, only 5 to 10 percent present themselves as being able to do "grrrrreeeeat things for the company and the team," and *those* are the 5 to 10 percent that get the interviews.

8. Set a Date to Stop Tinkering.

Eventually you need to finish your résumé (and your cover letter). So stop. Put your pencil down. Stop fine-tuning. Stop trying different versions. Accept that, at some point, you have hit a point of diminishing marginal returns[5] and need to stop polishing your résumé and start using it.

No one ever got a job by exclusively sitting behind a computer. Build your tools and go forth.

You can, and surely will, make tweaks based on feedback. But start using your résumé first. Get feedback from peers and mentors, start applying to jobs, and start networking. Finish up and move on. Seriously. This is important.

The Specific and Important Things to Know

So those few tips will give you something to think about as you approach your word processor and a blank screen. The following guidelines will help you with turning that blank screen into a compelling document.

---

[5] This is an excellent economic principle to adopt for many aspects of work and for consuming chocolate.

Basic Formatting

There is no single correct way to format a résumé. You can choose from plenty of free templates online or come up with your own. It's your résumé; you need to own the way it looks and what it says. I recommend staying away from colored paper, scents, and sending your résumé attached to a box of cookies, but as I said previously, this is all subjective.

For practical purposes, here are some generally accepted guidelines.

Layout

- Indicate your name, address, and contact information prominently at the top.
- After your contact information, you can add:
  - Your one- to two-sentence summary of who you are and what you are seeking.
  - A list of your most salable skills such as coding programs, language fluency, etc., under the heading "Skills." Don't add MS Office as that is assumed. If you know Advanced Excel that's okay. If you used PowerPoint in creating presentations at a job or internship, call that out as a presentation development skill in the relevant professional experience description.
  - Alternatively, you could list your most impressive accomplishments under the heading "Key Accomplishments," and include the names of the tools and/or skills you used.
- An Education section follows and includes your college, degree(s), relevant coursework if applicable to your search, awards, special projects such as a thesis, and any extracurricular achievements.
  - Include your GPA if 3.0 or above. Only write your GPA out to one place after the decimal point. Include your GPA in your major if higher, but if you do, be sure to include your overall GPA too.
  - The Education section should appear near the top of your

résumé when you are starting out, but then be moved to near the bottom once you have a little over five years of professional experience.

- After graduating from college, leave off high-school achievements unless they're very relevant to your story. Summer jobs can be important as they show your work ethic, continuity with a single employer, or otherwise support your "story" (interests, skills, objectives).

- After five to seven years out of college, leave off college activities and internships, unless they're particularly relevant.

- The "Professional" or "Experience" section is next. It lists the dates and descriptions of your employment, companies, and locations in chronological order starting with current or most recent.

  - If you worked while in college, this shows strong work ethic.

  - Concern yourself most with your recent accomplishments. A potential employer is less interested in what you did more than five years ago.

- Skills can come next if you are more comfortable placing them at the bottom, but I say, if you've got them, why not lead with them?

- Add a "Personal" or "Other" section last with a few personal details that may give insight into your outside-of-work life. The purpose of this is to potentially spark conversation and show an interviewer what you would be like to chat with every day in the office, as well as what kinds of things interest you. If you are an avid sports fan, reader, or film noir afficionado, here is where you want to mention it. Avoid politics and religion as these can be polarizing subjects to many people, but don't be afraid to talk about other interests.

Formatting

- Use bolding, underlining, bigger fonts, white space, and anything else you can to make the most impressive parts of your résumé stand out.
- You can set off examples of your best and most salable skills and credentials with bullet points.
- Within a category, you can make something stand out by tabbing it toward the middle.
- To save space, you can put lists into two columns.
- To get all the text to fit on one page, play with margins and font sizes. As mentioned previously, a two-page résumé is pretentious unless you have at least ten to fifteen years of professional experience. Stay at one page for as long as you possibly can.

Content

As for content, there are more schools of thought for basic layout and formatting than there are about where you can find the best pizza. The following section is less "generally accepted" and more "JobCoachAmy recommends." Having said that, these seven principles are decidedly market tested:

> **JerseyCoachAmy:** *"Market tested" is a nice way to say "This sh*t works, so why on earth would you not use it?"*

1. Present What You Have Accomplished, Not What You Did.

Being accountable for tasks and responsible for activities shows that you were involved in the fabric of an organization (e.g., you managed a lot of people or were a campus leader, depending on your career stage). But what did you accomplish? Add specifics about how you added value.

For example, did you

- meet or exceed your goals consistently?
- complete your tasks with 100 percent accuracy?
- take on the responsibilities for your manager after they left three months into your tenure?
- get promoted ahead of cycle?
- institute new processes that saved the company money or improved efficiency?
- launch a new product successfully that beat revenue projections?

What you accomplish, whatever it is, is more important than where you do it. Went to a highly prestigious school? Fantastic, make sure you did something more impressive than get accepted. Landed an internship at Google? Good for you! Prove on your résumé that you didn't spend your time getting coffee by stating what sort of value you provided while you were there. Any kind of initiative is excellent. An assignment of any sort is great if you completed it with an impact on the company's operations in any capacity (revenues? inventory? communications?) and indicates you developed an understanding of some aspect of the organization and its goals.

Similarly, a stellar record at any college is a good indicator that you are a hard worker who stands out amongst peers. Part-time work at a coffee shop, library, or lab may not be glamorous, but it shows that you are not afraid of hard work and probably learned something about customer service and working in teams. Accomplishing more than what was expected of you such as taking on a supervisory role, designing a system for training new employees, or tweaking a database to perform better is super impressive.

Any work is something of which you can be proud. But from a hiring manager's perspective, it's not an indication that you are awesome. Rather, it's an indication that you were given an opportunity. What did you do with it? The hiring manager is thinking, "If I give you an opportunity, what will you do for me?"

JerseyCoachAmy: *You needed to work a paying job and so could not take an internship over the summer? Me too. Work is work. Be proud of it, put it on your résumé, and point out if you did anything noteworthy or did something like kept a job while also going to school at night. Every manager wants someone with a strong work ethic and the ability to juggle multiple priorities. Get over yourself.*

If you are a Google intern, be the Google intern who resolved an algorithm issue that no one else could, or solved a challenge on your own initiative because you thought it could be improved. Be the employee, even the part-time after-school employee, who redesigned the way the café recorded or stored inventory. If you are working two jobs at the mall because you need to make as much money as you can, you are not at a disadvantage because you don't have a fancy internship.

Whatever your job is, try to take some initiative and make a mark. You want to be remembered for something other than your winning personality or quirky hobby. If you see a problem, ask your manager if you can try to fix it. You'll earn a good reference and some valuable experience. For example:

- Does it take too long to bring new people up to speed? Offer to make a document and video that replaces the bulk of the training.
- Does putting out new inventory take too long because the stock room is unorganized? Create a system.

- Do you keep getting asked the same question over and over by customers? Make a sign.

It doesn't have to be huge. Just spend some time thinking about it.

JerseyCoachAmy: *Let's face it, sometimes there is nothing you can do to make a change to a business—they don't want to hear it. Just noticing what makes a business run really well—or really poorly— is a good thing to understand and be able to talk about. You never want to act like you know more than the people who run the business where you worked, and you never throw shade. But showing that you understand what the business does well and what its challenges are shows you did more than show up every day and do what you were told, which is something. You can always talk about your improvement ideas even if you can't implement them so they can be added to your résumé.*

An impressive résumé is not necessarily a résumé that shows you've been able to land some cool roles. An impressive résumé is one that shows you have stood out and made a difference with whatever opportunities you have had. Try to make an impact wherever you land. Then quantify the impact on your résumé, as per below.

2. Be as Quantitative as Possible.

You need as many qualifying numbers as you can put in your résumé to give recruiters and hiring managers an idea of your accomplishments by order of magnitude—rough numbers are fine and so are estimates. For example:

- If you ran a campus organization, did the organization involve 15 people or 150? Was the budget $500 or $5,000?
- If you managed your company's intern program, were there 10 interns or 100?
- If you were selected for an award or special program, how many others were in the running?
- Was the P&L you had responsibility for at the Women in Business Club $1,000 or $10,000?
- Was the event you managed for 50 people with a budget of $2,500, or for 1,000 people with a budget of $50,000?
- Did you resolve an issue for a team of 3 or 30?
- Did the software bug you fixed reduce the soft launch time by 4 days or 4 weeks?
- When you worked cross-functionally, was it with 2 teams or 20?
- Did the database you queried every day for your thesis have 500 records or 500,000?

It all matters. Don't be discouraged if these questions, or this entire section, didn't inspire you to remember something you did that is résumé-worthy. Spend some time thinking about the skills you've outlined and the times you've used them. I've never worked with a client who didn't add something to their resume after going through these exercises.

JerseyCoachAmy: *Working in a donut shop? How many dozens were you moving weekly? How about approximate daily sales? Were you allowed to do the count-out? Same with pumping gas or sweeping a local store. I don't care what you did, you can find numbers.*

Here are some examples of where you can insert numbers to make your résumé more specific and, as a result, more powerful:

- How many students turned out for the blood drive you managed your senior year?
- What was the budget for the event you worked on as an intern?
- How many people were in the database you kept updated at your after-school job?
- How many people were considered for the award that you actually won?
- What were the average sales per day of the store where you worked? How many people worked on the shift you managed?
- Were you able to schedule a consistent number of sales calls each week during your internship?

Not every number is going to be important, but every role has some significant numbers, regardless of level or industry. You may not feel you did anything important, however, there are always metrics involved in any job or internship. For example, if you delivered meals, how many a week? Were you always on time? Did you get 100 percent good reviews? Think about it:

- Were you able to upsell some customers at your retail job?
- Were you able to upgrade and improve the filing system when they asked you to organize it?
- Did you start a new social media channel for an event or small business or project? What were the results? Can you quantify the percentage you grew followers by or the number of "likes" you got?

It makes sense to keep a notebook of what you do and accomplish in your next job, but in the meantime, really think about what you did correctly in the past and what you may have been praised for. My guess is, you can come up with something—and in fact, I've never seen anyone fail to find something that will make their résumé stronger.

As you go through your career, continue to keep track of these kinds of numbers and the wins you are getting. Many of your managers will ask you to write your own reviews. Another good use of this data is that it will give you a database of accomplishments, projects, and skills you learned to draw from at review time. Over the course of your career, having all this data available can be very valuable.

When I work with C-Suite executives, I will ask roughly fifty to sixty questions about the details of their past victories, trying to get at those numbers that define the scope of their work by budget, revenue, stock price, and operating improvements. They can generally only answer a few, because in general they don't remember and were not allowed to take proprietary internal documents with them when they changed firms. But they never thought they would forget the results that they generated, or that they would necessarily be looking for a new role outside the company where they generated those results. So they didn't keep track in a detailed way. These clients generally answer questions in ranges, which is fine. Numbers on résumés often need to stay purposely vague for privacy and legal issues. But knowing them and being able to speak to them can have an impact. So, start keeping track of details early. Doing it throughout your career is good habit to start early and will make a difference for you.

3. Resist the Urge to Choose Fancy over Clear.

Get out of the way of your inner-Hemingway. You want to develop prose that is clear, concise, and cogent. Less is always more. Use the fewest words on the page as possible while still making sense. I'm not going to lie, this is hard. So, when it comes to things like your favorite turn of phrase? Be prepared to kill it for plainer, shorter words that make the point more concisely.

Once you have a good, first draft, you are probably going to need to simplify and pare down what you have written. Even if you really like that perfect turn of phrase a lot, follow Stephen King's advice to aspiring writers from his memoir *On Writing*[6] and "Kill your darlings, kill your darlings, even when it breaks your egocentric little scribbler's heart, kill your darlings."[7] (You would not believe the hilarious, eloquent, and amazing turns of phrase that wound up on the cutting room floor of my office while writing this book. Trust me. Side. Splitting. Hilarity.)

Here's an example that integrates what we've learned so far.

Base information:

For two years, I served as a retail associate at a busy store at the mall after school and on most weekends. I exceeded my sales quota pretty much every month. We never had high theft rates because it was easy for me to catch people with all the mirrors in the store, which I did a good job of watching. During busy times, I could ring up customers quickly, and during slow times I stayed busy with cleaning or moving fixtures around to better show off new stock (staying busy made the time go faster). I usually trained part-time seasonal sales and inventory help, which I really enjoyed. I arrived on time, did not leave before my shift was over, and was happy to cover other shifts when people asked. The best part of the job was interacting with clients, and I thought it was cool to learn about national merchandising and fashion plans from corporate.

---

[6] Stephen King, *On Writing: A Memoir of the Craft* (New York: Charles Scribner & Sons, 2000), pg. 222

[7] Often attributed to Faulkner, the earliest known example of this phrase was actually from Arthur Quiller-Couch, King Edward VII Professor of English Literature-Cambridge University, in his 1914 lecture, "On Style," from his 1913–14 Cambridge lecture series *On the Art of Writing*. Forrest Wickman, Culture Editor, *Slate*, October 18, 2013, https://slate.com/culture/2013/10/kill-your-darlings-writing-advice-what-writer-really-said-to-murder-your-babies.html.

First Draft of Résumé for Retail Store Job:

Boca Grande Bikinis
Bikini Island, FL   Dates
Retail Associate
Exceeded sales quota during tenure. Demonstrated excellent sales skills during peak sales times, staying calm and efficient. During non-peak times, stayed busy by identifying ways to add value throughout the store. Every holiday and annual sale season, asked to train seasonal employees on register, antitheft, and inventory processes. Never cut corners on shifts and always willing to go the extra mile. Demonstrated excellent relationship development skills with customers and other team members. Enjoyed developing relationships with corporate.

In the case of this example, a quick message to the manager or generally remembering a few numbers can help you get to the details:

- "I remember one day at the store we did about 1,000 transactions when things were crazy busy, but that rarely happened. A typical day was usually a little more than half of that, so I'm going to conservatively estimate that we had slightly more than 600 transactions on a busy day."
- "I definitely saw a report that showed in one year we did $2 million in sales but lost $350K to theft, so I'm going to make a percentage out of that."

Final:

Retail Store Name
Location   Dates
Retail Associate

Exceeded sales quota consistently during employment. Additional accomplishments include being asked to train 3 to 6 seasonal employees annually, taking initiative during slow times, performing well during extremely busy and high-pressure periods (>600 transactions per day) and contributing to consistently low theft rates (<2 percent). Enjoyed developing relationships with customers, teammates, and corporate.

4. On Formatting.

Even though the goal is to make your résumé spare in style, you can make your strongest accomplishments and most relevant experience for the role to which you are applying stand out by using highlighting and bolding on the page's real estate to visually draw attention to the best parts of your background. This is a really good way to use your 7.4 seconds and can get you moved to the "further consideration pile." Examples of good things to highlight or bold:

- An excellent GPA
- Winning a particularly competitive award or prestigious and well-known honor
- A unique aspect of your background that is in perfect alignment with the job description

Note that this is only a powerful tool if it's used extremely sparingly.

JerseyCoachAmy: *Sometimes, vivid colors and bright formatting can work for a résumé. Sometimes, they can be just plain fatiguing. And sometimes, they just look unprofessional. If you "just gotta be you" by demonstrating your creativity and uniqueness, my advice would be to wait until you get called in for the interview. Dye your hair purple, but*

> *don't use purple résumé paper. This is 100 percent, pure subjective opinion on my part, but it is based on my years of experience as a hiring manager. Use as you wish.*

Similarly, a unique design may get your résumé spit out of a computerized screener that cannot read something too nontraditional. That said, a few stylistic additions are fine, especially for a creative role or company. I've seen a "Top Ten Reasons I Was Born to Work Here" list in a cover letter yield good results. A risk can sometimes strike the right tone at the right time for the right reviewer. Generally, however, recognize that going rogue is a risk. Creativity requires the luxury of having someone take the time to understand and appreciate your efforts, and time is not something recruiters or hiring managers have a lot of during this process.

5. Integrate the Three Credentials Every Employer Wants.

Attention to detail, the ability to juggle multiple priorities, and good organization skills are three skills that every hiring manager needs in every job, regardless of whether they are in the job description. We'll talk more about these skills when we review interviewing and the "stories" you want to develop about your background to showcase your best experiences. You'll want to integrate these three skills as highlights in all the stories you tell. For example:

- "In my internship, I became the person everyone came to for proofing code because I had the best eye for knowing when something didn't look right."
- "I was always the person in a group project who just naturally assumed the role of making sure that other people got their work

done on time. I like doing it, and I have a knack for not annoying people because they trust me to keep us on track."

- "I like waitressing. I perform best when I have a lot of things I need to get done at the same time and have to think on my feet to prioritize what needs to be done."

For now, we'll think about these three skills in the context of just a line or two for your résumé.

- Attention to detail. Because small mistakes can have big consequences and make everyone one look bad.
  - If you can prove on your résumé and in your interview that you are an extra line of defense before something goes out the door, such as a wrong number or typo that could have repercussions for your manager, you can increase your chances of getting hired.
    - *Example:* Responsible for reviewing all customer credit card applications before they went on to the first step of processing to be sure that required details were available and had been filled in correctly. One hundred percent accuracy in moving applications to next step.
- The ability to juggle multiple priorities. Because you are inevitably going to need to do a lot of things at once.
  - Everyone has the experience of three or four senior colleagues showing up at their door at the same time and asking for something to be done in the next five minutes. If you can demonstrate that this is not a new experience for you and that you've mastered the art of separating out which one *really* has an immediate need and from the ones that can wait without having a melt down, then you may be a little closer to getting that offer.
    - *Example:* Accountable for supporting a fundraising team

of 3 during an event involving 6 vendors, 150 guests, a budget of $2,500, and a donation goal of $300,000. All goals were met. Managed day-of-event details with no breakdowns in guest experience or critical follow-up to donation pledges.

- Organization skills. If you're not organized, you're not likely to be as productive as someone who is organized.

  - Imagine you are a manager, and you need a third-quarter number for *your* boss. You show up at the cubby of one of your direct reports, William, to ask for the number. William looks through a few piles on his desk, overturns several papers on the floor and eventually tells you he will bring the number to you in about five minutes. Now, imagine you show up at Kelsey's cubby asking for the same number and she hits two keystrokes, and you walk away with your number fifteen seconds later. William may be brilliant, but sometimes all you need is an employee who is organized.

    - *Example*: Intern responsibilities included organizing weekly lunches for inside sales team of 18 and managing related expenses, conducting follow-up on all items requested by field staff of 50 (as many as 100 requests/week), and turning around expense reporting for 2 regions (12 outside reps) in 36 hours.

Think hard about where and how you have exhibited these three traits. Most clients have great stories that don't occur to them at first. Work the fact that you have these skills into your résumé and, eventually, your interview if you can.

6. The One-Page, Two-Page Issue.

Résumés should be one page until you are at least ten years into your career. If you must, you can prepare a separate document that lists the types of projects you have completed, or cases you've worked on, or products you have launched to bring to an interview, but do not submit it with your application. If you want to switch from a for-profit career to a mission-driven organization and only have volunteer experience in mission-driven organizations, you can make a supplemental page for your résumé with volunteer experience. However, early in your career you really need to condense your résumé to one page or assume that most people are not going to look at your second page. Some internal recruiters and hiring managers will even throw away two-page résumés from young candidates unless the second page is specifically a list of publications or patents.

7. Should It Stay or Should It Go? Some Guidelines.

Here are some general rules of thumb for identifying whether something can stay or go from your résumé. Ask yourself the following. Does this

- use accessible terminology (i.e., no acronyms for departments or programs);
- demonstrate my impact on the company's overall ability to serve its customers or improve its profitability;
- show initiative rather than me doing assignments;
- have any bearing on what I want to do in my next role and my career;
- demonstrate my ability to perform well in my current or past roles;
- indicate my ability to perform well in the role to which I am applying;
- make me stand out from other candidates?

You should be able to answer yes to at least one of these. If your margins are already narrow and your font size is 10 (meaning: you need to pare things down but shouldn't make the margins or font any smaller), go through the list again and toss the items that only have one yes answer until things fit.

Most of these questions are role-specific and may have "yes" answers for certain applications and not for others, so use relevance in your screening as well. For example, this question:

- Demonstrate my ability to perform well in my current or past roles?

If you are applying for an entry-level role in pharmaceutical sales, your volunteer work at a hospital would be relevant as it shows an interest in health care and indicates that you have already spent time in the medical world. If you are applying for an entry-level role in data security (often referred to by its category name, SaaS, or software as a service), sales then you can probably leave off that volunteer work to gain space.

> **JerseyCoachAmy:** *Also, don't use big words: you'll look like you're trying too hard. Don't puff up anything to sound like something (hiring managers can tell). Imagine your most sarcastic friend reading your résumé, and if they would skewer you for something, take it out.*

Low- and High-Impact Résumé Examples

Following are two examples of a new grad's low-impact résumé turned into a high-impact résumé using the guidelines outlined in this chapter. The first résumé is for a client with a strong academic track record and summer jobs that she did not think added much to her profile. She was seeking a business role while she considered graduate school. We talked about specific skills she developed while in college and during her summer roles and how they would help her find a professional entry-level position in a life sciences firm, which she did fairly quickly with her new résumé.

The second résumé is for a client who was interested in a department store's retail training program, but who did not have a lot of retail in his background. His résumé, too, benefitted from calling out his accomplishments and adding quantitative parameters to prove that he could handle the basics of what he would have to learn in retail: working with customers, staying calm when things become a little crazy or very fast-paced, becoming familiar with financial transactions, and understanding how to upsell to customers. With his new résumé, he quickly got an interview for several training programs.

Additional cover letter and résumé examples can be found in the workbook available on www.jobcoachamy.com/shop.

Low-Impact Résumé 1

Address   Mobile
City, Town   Email

EDUCATION

Philadelphia University,
College of Arts & Sciences, Philadelphia, Pennsylvania   2018
- Bachelor of Science in Biology
- Relevant Coursework: Physiology, Microbiology, Genetics, Histology, Organic Chemistry

Knights High School, Location   2014

PROFESSIONAL EXPERIENCE

Enterprise Bank & Trust Co., Landings, Pennsylvania   20014–2018
- Small Business Loan Representative—Generated beneficial people skills, helped customers feel at ease, adapted to work quickly and efficiently, easily learned new procedures and software programs, observed financial aspects of commercial businesses
- Customer Service Representative—Processed personal and commercial banking transactions for customers, traveled to various branches on an as-needed basis, quickly adapted to new surroundings while forging relationships with new colleagues in the process

EXTRACURRICULAR ACTIVITIES

Olympics Festival (largest college event in the United States), Volunteer
Students Against Breast Cancer, Active Member & Fundraiser
- Organized the Relay for Life team
- Volunteered and raised money for free mammogram clinics in Philadelphia

COMMUNITY SERVICE

St. Mary Parish Soup Kitchen, Volunteer and Youth Ministry Leader
Knights Community Exchange Food Pantry

ATHLETICS

Knights High School
- Varsity Field Hockey
- Varsity Lacrosse
- Varsity Swimming

PERSONAL

Travel, Literature, Cooking, Hiking, and Playing/Coaching Athletics

High-Impact Résumé 1

NAME
Address   Mobile phone
Landings, Pennsylvania   email

Seeking entry-level role in a life-sciences related organization that will leverage my research, project management, and team skills.

ACCOMPLISHMENTS
- Graduated with 3.4 GPA after switching majors (Chemistry to Biology), which required double course-load
- Identified, researched, and presented a senior thesis linking global warming to the exponential growth of insects; included significant data collection and modeling to support conclusion
- Worked summers in a high-pressure, customer service intensive environment working on small business loan products; learned to follow detailed processes, develop relationships in high-pressure situations, and keep close attention to detail for accurate data capture
- Natural leader: repeatedly voted captain of multiple sports teams during high school

EDUCATION
Philadelphia University,
College of Arts & Sciences, Philadelphia, Pennsylvania   2018
- Bachelor of Science in Biology—relevant coursework included Physiology, Microbiology, Genetics, Histology, Organic Chemistry

Knights High School, Landings, Pennsylvania   2014

PROFESSIONAL EXPERIENCE
Enterprise Bank & Trust Co., Landings, Pennsylvania   2014–2018
- Small Business Loan Representative
- Customer Service Representative

EXTRACURRICULAR ACTIVITIES
Pre-Dental Student Association, Co-Founder
Special Olympics Festival Volunteer
Students Against Breast Cancer, Active Member & Fundraiser
- Organized the Relay for Life team
- Volunteered and raised money for free mammogram clinics in Philadelphia

COMMUNITY SERVICE
St. Mary Parish Soup Kitchen, Volunteer and Youth Ministry Leader
Knights Community Exchange Food Pantry

ATHLETICS
Knights High School
- Varsity Field Hockey Program
- Varsity Lacrosse
- Varsity Swimming

PERSONAL
Interested in travel, literature, cooking, hiking, and playing/coaching athletics

Low-Impact Résumé 2

Address.   Phone
Address   Email

Objective:
To secure a position that will allow for the growth of my business and leadership skills.

Education:
Maine State University, Portland, ME   May 2018
Bachelor of Arts in Business
Concentration in Entrepreneurship

Down East Community College, Ogunquit, ME   May 2016
Associate of Arts in Liberal Arts
Corey College, Peabody, ME   September 2014–May 2015

Work Experience:
Duke's Salon and Spa
Peabody, ME—Salon Coordinator/Assistant   March 2015–Present
- Assist stylists on salon floor
- Attend to clients, i.e., scheduling and processing transactions
- Updated social media/marketing systems

Simon & Associates—Family Law Office   May 2014–Present
North Reading, ME—Receptionist/Office Assistant
- Scheduled client appointments
- Answered multi-line phone system
- Provided administrative support in a fast-paced environment
- Operated office equipment, i.e., computer, copy/fax, and printers

Bed Bath and Beyond   May 2013–July 2014
York, ME—Sales Associate
- Appointed bridal consultant by choice of management
- Received award for most sales of "product of the month"
- Provided assistance to customers and worked as a cashier

Skills/Qualifications:
- Proficient in Microsoft Office including Word, Excel, and PowerPoint
- Ability to prioritize tasks in a timely manner
- Capability to work in a team structure and collaborate with others
- Independently self-motivated and detail-oriented

High-Impact Résumé 2

Address.   Phone
Address   Email

To combine my passion for the retail industry with my sales and relationship skills through an entry-level position with growth opportunities.

Education:

Maine State University, Portland, ME   May 2018
Bachelor of Arts in Business
Concentration in Entrepreneurship

Work Experience:

Simon & Associates—Family Law Office   May 2014–Present
South Reading, ME—Receptionist/Office Assistant
- Performed general administrative support and client interface for this very fast-paced environment of 12 attorneys, handling up to ten cases each simultaneously
- Received consistently high marks for professionalism in working with clients going through stressful personal situations, as well as for being efficient and effective with office technology and systems
- Quickly mastered highly detailed and rigorous nature of legal filings, documentation, and procedures

Duke's Salon and Spa
Peabody, ME—Salon Coordinator/Assistant   March 2015–Present
- Structured, executed, and measured salon's first social media campaigns across all major digital platforms: branding, promotions, and style posts accounted for approximately 10 % increase in new client sales and driving 3 to 6 additional walk-ins per week
- Accountable for supporting 4 to 6 professionals and up to 28 clients daily for service prep; insuring work areas are clean, well-organized, and fully stocked for upcoming services; managing additional requests as needed
- Handle scheduling up to 60 client appointments per 8-hour shift, as well as up to 40 financial transactions for services and product (cash and credit)
- Recognized regularly by clients as key team member contributing to retention, relationship

Bed, Bath and Beyond   May 2013–July 2014
York, ME—Sales Associate, Bridal Consultant
- After only six weeks, given incremental accountability for driving sales when selected by Management as store Bridal Consultant. Developed relationships with couples selecting registries and encouraged them to increase their selections across departments.
- Awarded highest monthly sales recognition for regional product promotion ("Product of the Month")

Qualifications:

- Strong work ethic; worked approximately 20 hours per week while finishing college degree
- Highly self-motivated, detail-oriented, and passionate about achieving goals
- Extremely productive and able to prioritize tasks in a timely manner
- Skilled at working in teams and collaborating with colleagues

Your LinkedIn Profile

You should have a good LinkedIn profile that generally matches your written résumé. LinkedIn has become the standard for job seekers, recruiters, and potential employers. Invest a little time in your profile by adding interests, joining groups, and asking for recommendations. There is really no downside.

> **JerseyCoachAmy:** *The LinkedIn software is pretty much idiot-proof. Click the pencil to cut and paste your résumé into their format. They do a lot of the work for you to serve up potential networking contacts, affinity groups, and even people who might be able to provide you with references. Pay attention. Follow the companies where you apply. Watch what they post. This does not require business wizardry on your part; it requires a little time and attention.*

When completing your professional online profile, you'll need two additional pieces of information:

- A short, one-line summary of who you are as a professional
- A longer, but still brief, summary of your career expertise and interests

Rather than providing you with examples that may not be relevant, I encourage you to look up people you know and people with titles (again, the search function is excellent on the platform) that you may someday want to have. Look at what they have written for summaries and use their examples as guidelines.

Hopefully, I do not need to tell you to clean up the other aspects of your online profile: Google yourself and take the results seriously. And do it regularly. Think about doing this on a regular basis during the year whether you are looking for a job or not.

Most people in the recruiting process will look at your LinkedIn profile as you get closer to getting an offer. This may be out of simple curiosity about what a potential colleague is like or it may be for solid professional reasons, such as to see if you've shared articles on the topic about which you claim to be knowledgeable and passionate. In either case, you want to make sure that your résumé syncs up as closely as possible with your profile so there is no new or different information.

Think about this from a potential employer's point of view. You want to present your best self on both platforms because, to an employer, why would they differ? They may wonder, "Could you be conducting different job searches? Or could you just be lazy—you only bother to update your résumé and not your LinkedIn profile?" Neither is a good signal to send to a potential employer.

You'll want to put a link to your LinkedIn profile in your email signature for both recruiting and networking purposes. You can put a live LinkedIn link in your résumé header, although in my experience most people print out résumés for reference so a link on the page isn't always helpful. If you are going to add a link, get an abbreviation or even make your name a live hyperlink. In other words, don't consume all the space that a full link entails.

Between the Lines of Your Résumé

In general, a potential employer will be most interested in what you are doing now, the skills you've been developing, and what your track record has been. As such, you want your résumé to answer the following questions at a glance, or be prepared to address them in an interview:

1. Have you stayed at a reasonable amount of time in each role and do the dates indicate that you left of your own accord from each

organization rather than at someone else's request? If not, are you prepared to address the question?

2. Does each job change represent an increase in responsibility (supervisory duties, accounts, resources, profit and loss accountability, etc.)?

3. Was something accomplished in each role (meeting goals, successfully completing projects, establishing money-saving processes, rolling out revenue enhancing campaigns or product enhancements, etc.)?

Even when you are just starting out, there are ways to indicate an increasing amount of accountability in, for example, a school organization (e.g., becoming an officer) or a part-time retail job (e.g., assigned shift scheduling for all part-time staff). Increasing accountability indicates a level of strong character that will make for a good employee, so include whatever detail you can to show that this is something that you have been awarded.

That said, once you have three to five years of professional experience, that should speak for itself, and you don't have to go reaching back to college or before that to prove that you are hardworking and dedicated. Once you have one or two "wins" in your professional life, you can start to reduce the detail you previously shared about your college leadership and internship experience to focus on the more recent accomplishments.

As you will see in the next chapter, your cover letter will follow many of these same principles. Your cover letter, like your résumé, will highlight the strongest elements of your background. These will later become the backbone of your interview strategy as well.

Summary

- Your résumé must be extremely focused, as you need to prepare for some tough technical and human hurdles. Use the tricks presented here to make your résumé spare in style but impactful in effect:

- Focus on accomplishments, not tasks.
- Use numbers when you can, not to be precise but to provide an order of magnitude. Selling five cups of lemonade a day at your stand is different from selling five hundred.
- Use simple language. Don't be wordy.
- Your résumé should only be one page in length unless you have been in the workplace for at least a decade.
- Details matter. Typos can get you rejected, as can a file name that gets you put in another folder by accident. Be aware.
- Your résumé can't help you until you start using it. Set a "stop" date for tinkering with your résumé and move on to other job search tasks.
- Make sure your LinkedIn profile matches your résumé. LinkedIn can help you, so you want to make sure it has the best and most current version of your résumé.
- Styles differ, but basic mechanics do not. Use the style that best represents you, but make sure your résumé is simple enough to get the key data across with ease. If a reader (i.e., recruiter or hiring manager or third-party talent acquisition agent) doesn't understand your résumé, the easiest course of action for them will be to eliminate it from consideration and move on to the three hundred-plus behind it.
- Look for what your résumé is saying about you between the lines. For example, if you worked for a landscaper during the day and waited tables at night during your college summers, then you are very familiar with hard work and customer service. Every job matters—whether it is scooping ice cream, folding sweaters, or writing code.

Chapter 6.
Develop a High-Impact Cover Letter

You may ask, "Amy, if I only have 7.4 seconds to make an impression, why should I send a cover letter? Don't I want to draw attention immediately to my résumé where everything is presented clearly and succinctly?" It's a fair question. Here's my answer:

A cover letter is a second chance to make a first impression. You have a chance to summarize your best qualities but also add *why* you are interested in this role, *why* you would be able to perform the required responsibilities well and *why* want to join the company. Those are important messages. And you can't really say any of those things in a résumé.

In an initial screen, having no cover letter may not hurt you. A bad cover letter *will* hurt you. A good cover letter may help or may be neutral.

If you make it *past* the first screen, the cover letter becomes much more important. If a cover letter was an option and you don't provide one, it looks like you may have applied quickly without a lot of thought. This is not good—maybe you are not as interested in the job as the candidates who took the time to write cover letters. If your cover letter stands out (i.e., is high impact) it can make difference between making it through the first screen and getting an interview. It matters. That is my opinion, albeit one that is based on many years of data.

> **JerseyCoachAmy:** *Jump at the chance to send a cover letter if the company will let you submit one. If you can write a concise letter, you can write a concise business memo, and I don't have to be the recipient of all your long, wordy project summaries that read like a college English paper. I like you better already.*

These are the guiding principles I use with my clients that have proven most successful and are based on my experience as a hiring manager:

- Always try to send cover letters. They offer an opportunity to make yourself memorable and present a second chance to make a first impression. In other words, cover letters are an opportunity to catch the eye of a decision-maker.
- Make cover letters short, otherwise no one is going to read them.
- *Make cover letters short, otherwise no one is going to read them.* This bears repeating.
- Like with your résumé, create a cover letter template that is easily replicable.
- Do a little research for each application's cover letter, so that the content is focused on the opportunity and is specific to the company.

Beyond that, here's what is worth learning in greater detail.

The Generally Important Things to Know

- Always submit a customized cover letter if you can. The opportunity is to catch someone's attention by highlighting the specific reasons you will add value in this job so that the recruiter becomes interested enough to learn more about you as a candidate.

- Cover letters are not a vehicle for writing an essay about your personal history, hopes, or dreams. They indicate you didn't randomly upload your résumé to apply to every job you could find online (a.k.a. "spraying and praying"), but that you are genuinely interested enough to take the time to craft a letter explaining your interest in the role to which you are applying.

- Cover letters are considered good by recruiters, other human resource professionals, and hiring managers when they indicate you have taken a little time to research the company and can convey your genuine interest. A good cover letter will get those ideas across clearly and concisely.

- Cover letters are good for you when they are replicable. Just like dating, job searching is a numbers game. You are going to want to get out a lot of applications to increase your odds of getting an interview, and you can't spend lots of time starting from scratch for each application. The answer is to create a letter that is roughly 80 percent template and 20 percent customized for a particular position. My recommendation for that 20 percent? Customize 10 percent of it to indicate how you can add value in the role and the other 10 percent to demonstrate your interest in the organization.

- No one is going to read a cover letter that is long and wordy. Nor do you have the time to craft a unique masterpiece for each application. Unlike writing college papers or letters to significant others, an elegant turn of phrase or well-thought-out metaphor does not make you stand out from other candidates in a good way. Writing a cover letter like a college thesis makes recruiters' eyes glaze over. The more words on the page, the more difficult it becomes to see the ones that matter, like your relevant experience for and sincere interest in the role. See the difference between using lengthy prose versus using concise, high-impact language in the example below.

- *Lengthy prose*: "In my first few years out of college while I was working at a medical insurance call center, I realized that I liked working with customers. What I did not like was telling them where else they needed to call to resolve their inquiry or dispute rather than being able to resolve the issue myself. It was great to hear their stories and navigate the system to help them, but I did not enjoy just sending them on and not hearing if their issues were resolved. So, I am applying to this role with great hope that I will be able to work with customers not only to learn what issues they are having with your software product, but also to be able to navigate those issues and resolve them all within the scope of my own role."

- *Concise, High Impact Language:* "I have enjoyed working for several years in a customer care center helping to identify how to resolve issues and disputes. Currently, I am seeking a role where I can apply my skills to working with customers from issue identification through to resolution."

    Makes a difference, right?

• Use your completed résumé and cover letter wisely. *Updating your LinkedIn profile is all the marketing you should be doing with your résumé.* I know, almost every job board will ask you to upload your résumé publicly for anyone to see. Don't do it: you will be most likely to attract the wrong kind of attention, and you lose control of your candidacy as soon as you post. You have a LinkedIn profile and you are easy to find there.

- *The companies* that are looking in online aggregated résumé pools are likely going to offer you the kind of job you don't want: making cold calls, handing out surveys in malls on the weekend, or performing "disruption marketing" by passing out free samples on the street. (Starting your career that way can really impress future employers because it is hard and honest work. However, you may find the work too hard.)

- *The third-party recruiters* who are looking in those résumé pools may not be the kind of recruiters you want to attract. (See the accompanying workbook: About Third-Party Recruiters for more information.) The important thing to know is that if a third-party recruiter puts you in front of an organization (versus that organization receiving your application directly from you), you automatically become more expensive.

• Many company websites will also encourage you to send in your résumé so they can keep you in mind until something becomes available. This is fine to do as a demonstration of interest but will not be a very effective as a job search tactic. I would not rely on anyone getting back to you based on a résumé sent in as a general expression of interest unless you are a unicorn with a specific skill that is hard to find or in high demand. A more effective tactic would be to set an alert for roles at that company as they become available and apply specifically to that role.

• Once you have applied to a role, you are going to want to do everything you can to get your résumé forwarded to the hiring manager or the human resources department inside the company. (See the next chapter on networking.)

• Lastly, be sure to keep a record of every company and organization where you have applied, as well as the date, the file of the documents you submitted and, if applicable, any contacts you made. I guarantee you'll want to reference your records at some point.

JerseyCoachAmy: *You'll be tempted to send out a bunch of résumés without cover letters. The official term for this practice in the biz is* *"spraying and praying." Is it possible for this to pay off? Sure. Are you going to hear of someone who sprayed and prayed and got a job just fine? Of course, you are. Can a unicorn walk into your kitchen at any time and deliver you a basket of puppies? Same odds.*

The Specific and Important Things to Know

- Follow traditional letter writing conventions for your cover letter including the date, your contact information, and the company headquarters address, as well as a reference to the role to which you are applying.
- The job title and job code, if available, need to be called out in the subject line. This represents a safeguard in case the file is printed out and gets mixed up with applications for other roles. For example:

Date
Mary W. Conlon
Senior Vice President
Artemis Analytics
100 Advent Street
Boston, Massachusetts

- Re: Quantitative Analyst, Job Code 117_04

- Only use the zip code if you are using USPS and not electronic delivery. I also prefer no abbreviations for street or state names, but that is also *my* rule and not *a* rule.
- In the first paragraph, mention something specific about the organization, position, or industry. My recommendation is to

thank the reader for considering your candidacy. Include how you can add value based on the skills you already have and be as specific as possible. This should not be a long introduction—three to four sentences should do.

- Next, provide an overview of your skills and experience that supports your statement, preferably using bullet points or some other extremely simple-to-read format. These can be your skills, stated with examples, or maybe the three to four strongest experiences from your résumé that support your candidacy.

- The closing paragraph should reiterate your interest. Mention something specific about why you are excited about this particular role or this particular industry—perhaps that you are interested in the kinds of projects that the company does or why you love its products or its client work. A quick review of the company's website will tell you what they value and, in turn, give you some ideas for what to focus on.

- You don't need to do a lot of research on the role or the organization, just some preliminary review. We'll go into much greater depth about how to analyze both a company and a job description in Chapter 8. If you get called into an interview, you'll want to do more follow up.

- Explain any logistics also in the closing paragraph (e.g., "Currently living in Philadelphia but will be moving to New York [where the job is] in three weeks."), and that you would be thrilled to move forward in the process. Thank them here, if you have not done so already, for reviewing your candidacy.

- Keep it to one page.

- Use lots of white space.

- Use lots of bolding and underlining to focus on the key points you think important.

- Make everything but the address, subject line, and parts of the first and last paragraphs fully templated.

- Put your cover letter and résumé in one file: recruiters and hiring managers don't want to have to keep track of two electronic files for you. Include your name and contact information on all pages. My preference is to repeat your email or cell phone again under the signature line, and to put your name and all contact information in the header.
- As mentioned in Chapters 4 and 6, do not name the file for your own convenience. Name the file for the convenience of those at the organization. For example, most people name their résumés with their last name and the date last updated, e.g., Conlon_December2018. But let's say I'm the hiring manager and I interviewed a dozen candidates for a role that was placed on hold a month ago, and now I'm trying to remember who I liked and who I didn't. Maybe I have a big résumé folder on my desk, but I can't remember the names of the people I interviewed a month ago for a role. What I *do* remember is the position title or code. So do me a favor and name your file Conlon_Jobcode11704 or Conlon_QuantAnlst, and you just may improve your chances of being found when I am looking for you.
- Assume the recipient is going to print out your file as well as email it to colleagues. Ensure your cover letter and résumé formatting look like they go together, and the cover letter references the résumé as an attachment in case they get separated.
- Spell check. Twice. Have a friend read your final draft as an extra step. Having a typo of any sort is an easy excuse for someone to reduce the pile by one more and eliminate yours.
- Time is of the essence when submitting a job application: the longer a job is posted, the more résumés come in, and the less attention yours is likely to get.
- Applying to jobs is a numbers game from the perspective of *when* your file is submitted as well. Getting your résumé in early

is both a good thing from a process perspective (late entrants get buried) and to prove your enthusiasm.[1]

- Once you get the hang of it, customizing every letter for each job and organization will not take a lot of time. You can then go back and input key words from the job description into your cover letter and résumé to try and get it flagged in early screening.
- Don't talk yourself out of applying for something—take the swing even if it might be a miss. It's not that much work. You never know.

Creating a High-Impact Cover Letter Template—Some Examples

You can spend six to eight hours crafting every letter perfectly every time you apply for a job, but because it is a guarantee that no one is going to look at your masterpiece for more than six to eight seconds: why bother? An 80/20 template will allow you to get as many applications as possible out there, and that will increase your odds of getting interviewed.

My recommendation, as outlined above, is that your cover letter be in three parts. The following breaks down each of those parts and provides examples. I also provide a full example template that gives you guidelines for creating your own.

1. An introduction expressing why you know you can add value in the role based on your skills and the needs of the role (based on your understanding of the job description)
2. A bullet pointed, or otherwise very easy to read, list of your strongest experiences, which can be pulled from your résumé
3. A closing paragraph that demonstrates your specific interest in the organization

[1] This is important; we'll return to it in the interviewing section.

1. An introduction expressing why you know you can add value in the role based on your skills and the needs of the role (based on your understanding of it from the job description)

Convey your gratitude for being considered for the role, then focus on what you can do for the organization in the role <u>specifically</u>. The first paragraph of your cover letter should answer the question "How will you add value in the role? Based on what skills and experience?" Don't say how great you are in general. For example:

- Good message: "I believe I can quickly add value to the team, as I am experienced in working collaboratively between departments and on tight deadlines." (Note: this assumes that collaborative, cross-department work and tight deadlines are mentioned in the job description.)
- Not so good: "I have a lot of great skills and am a hard worker."

Example first paragraph:

"Thank you in advance for considering my application for the available Assistant Project Manager position. I am confident that I can add value in this role based on my experience to date as a proven hard worker with a strong track record of meeting or exceeding goals in the workplace. I am focused on obtaining a role of this type to start what I hope will be, a long career in property management, as I know my skills will allow me to excel in the industry. You will find that I have a strong work ethic and enjoy taking the initiative to make sure jobs are completed well, on time, and to the satisfaction of all involved."

2. A bullet-pointed list of your strongest experiences, which can be pulled from your résumé

Stating the strongest aspects of your background in your cover letter means you are doing all you can to double your chances of getting through the early rounds by having someone see "the good stuff" up front. You're basically taking the best aspects of your résumé and serving them up like an appetizer to make someone want to look at the full picture (i.e., the attached résumé). Hopefully, that will put you on the short list for further consideration. For example:

- Strong summary: Bullet point the skills of which you are most proud and that are most relevant, then align the experience where you were able to develop and practice those skills. For example,
  - Excellent written and verbal communication skills—Twice selected to create and deliver presentations during annual sports banquet; wrote and published several campus sports articles and national sports opinion pieces each year while in school.
- Weaker summary:
  - Campus newspaper 2018 to 2020, Sports Contributor

Example second section:

As you will see from the enclosed résumé, highlights of my experience to date include:

- Customer service focus, attention to detail and ability to perform well under pressure earned from working in high-turnover, high-pressure, retail environments (*Loews 2015 to Present, Baltimore Orioles Seasonal 2007 to 2009*)
- Success in all undertakings, including stint as four-year varsity

starting goalie for conference winning Division I NCAA soccer team *(Wembley College, Class of 2020)*, and success as a camp counselor for disabled kids and young adults *(Camp Minnesoot, 2007 to 2011)*

- Detailed process, data entry, and record keeping work associated with office administration as the result of a development internship focused on both fundraising and event planning *(Athletic Administration Intern, Rutgers Athletic Development, Summer 2016)*

- Exemplary work ethic and consistent history of enjoying physically demanding and fast-paced work through high school and college, including: landscaping, shipping and receiving, and aligning merchandising plans with retail installations

3. A closing paragraph that demonstrates your specific interest in the organization

As you end the letter, include specifics regarding why you are interested in the role and what you like about the company. *Make sure* you understand what the company does and how the role fits into the overall organization (an overall, general understanding is fine). If you can't figure it out, *ask* friends and family and search the Internet. *Keep asking* until you can answer the question conversationally. Within your closing paragraph, insert something specific about the organization about which the company is proud and features on their website. For example:

- Applying for a role at Nike? Mention part of the reason why you would love to work at Nike is their new product technology or their commitment to corporate responsibility.
- Want to work at a marketing services, environmental technology, or management consulting firm? Mention how one of the case studies you found on their website really made an impact on you. Or how their client list is exciting, and you are really

impressed with one or two of their specific campaigns (they will have examples on their website.) If, for example, you are applying to work at the ad agency that you know handles the PepsiCo account, a good example of mentioning something the company is proud of would be to reference the very engaging ad you've seen on national television that is linked to displays you've seen in your local grocery stores. A lesser example would be to reference the fact that they work in print, television, and digital channels.

Example closing paragraph:

It would be a great privilege to add my skills and experience to your team to help support your goals of expanding your corporate presence nationally. It would be an honor to support your enhanced building technology and environmental compliance services to customers. My experience in developing customer relationships and the service focus I have gained in my personal and campus roles will allow me to add value quickly. I hope to have the opportunity to further present my candidacy to you.

> **JerseyCoachAmy:** *If you take the easy route, plan to get busted. Think of companies like your friends who were in middle school band. If you say you want to work for a company, you'd better have a good reason as to why, otherwise your application is unlikely to make it all the way. It's just like when you told your friends in middle school band that you went to their Spring Fling concert, but they would quiz you anyway on what songs you liked best to make sure you didn't spend the concert in the parking lot on your phone. Companies and tween musicians do not mess around.*

The 80/20 Cover Letter Template
*(Customization elements in **bold**)*

Name
Phone and Email
Street Address (No Abbreviations)
City, State (No Abbreviations, No Zip)
Date

Recruiting (Name, if possible, or convention of your choice)
Company Name
Company Address (No Abbreviations)
City, State (No Abbreviations, No Zip unless sending via USPS)

Date, 20XX

Re: **Reference position title and, if available, job code**

Dear **Recruiter,**

Thank you in advance for considering my application for the above-referenced role. I know that I would be able to quickly add value in this role based on **my exceptional research and analytic skills, which have provided me with a strong track record of academic and professional success in the health care field.** My goal is to now **leverage my skills into a financial services role where I can continue to focus on demanding and detailed work outside of an academic setting.** As you will see from the attached résumé, I bring the following credentials:

- **2019 *cum laude* graduate from the College of Richmond (GPA 3.2), thesis in Biology**
- **Proven capabilities to learn quickly, find and interpret complex data, and communicate findings both concisely and**

precisely *(two years of research experience including conducting psychological research)*

- **Organization and time-management skills** *(currently working with several clinical research trials)*

My interest in this role is **to have the opportunity to continue to thrive in situations that require thoughtful analysis, quick problem solving, and clear writing. However, I would like to apply these skills to the field of financial services so that I can also leverage my interpersonal skills.** I hope to one day be in the position to provide **name of firm's** clients with the best possible **strategies for success by leveraging the quantitative analysis skills I have gained to date.**

I would be excited to discuss the **analyst** position with you. Thank you for your consideration of my application.

Sincerely,

Name
Résumé Attached

You'll find additional examples of cover letters and résumés in the companion workbook available on my website www.jobcoachamy.com/shop.

When a Cover Letter Isn't Enough

Increasingly, the application process does not stop after the résumé and cover letter are uploaded. Some online applications go a little further and ask you a series of questions. The purpose of these questions is to learn more about you before they make a decision as to whether they should invest time interviewing you. Typically, these questions are aimed at identifying the characteristics that make individuals a good fit within the organization. They also tell screeners a little bit more about the whole person. These questions generally fall into three categories:

- Get to know you: What gets you out of bed in the morning?
- Cultural fit: How do you see yourself fitting in here?
- Skills: Tell us about a time you (used Python on a project, or ran a social media campaign, or used your sales skills to change someone's mind) and what the impact was.

First, yes, you do need to input an answer to these questions. Second, no, you don't need to answer them right away. If you needed to create an account for an application or even if you just entered the company's domain to upload your résumé and cover letter, you can back out and think about how to answer the additional questions. Third, as with all aspects of the job search process, I recommend you apply some strategy in answering these questions.

Answering Get-to-Know-You Questions:

- These are not-so-thinly-veiled cultural-fit questions, so you may as well be as honest as possible. Hopefully, you can honestly say that what gets you out of bed is doing a good job at work and working hard to be rewarded. However, there is value in being honest: want to work to earn enough to retire with a house on the beach? Give your kids the advantages you did or did not have? Honesty is always the best option.
- **Example answer:**
  - "What gets me out of bed in the morning is the idea that I am going to work at a place where I can do a good job, be well liked, and be rewarded long- term for my family's sake."

Answering Cultural-Fit Questions:

- Companies that have these questions uppermost on their minds usually give away all the clues you need on their website. If their values are important to them, you'll find them clearly stated somewhere publicly. Craft an answer about how you personally align with those values (hopefully, it's closely) and how you will carry that into the workplace.
- **Example answer:**
  - "I really appreciate that you state working at your company requires a learner's mindset because the organization is constantly looking for ways to do things more efficiently and effectively. I see myself fitting in as a member of the marketing team who will always be willing to meet with operations, logistics, manufacturing, or sales to discuss new and better ways to work together and serve the customer."

Answering Skills Questions:

Use an example from your background that fits with the skill that is asked of you. Rarely will you be asked to give little more than a 2–3-sentence summary. You don't have to write an essay, because they don't have time to read an essay. Try this formula:

- Mention the skill.
- Mention the goal of the project you used it for.
- Mention your role, and something about the size of the project (number of people, budget, length of time—ballpark any number).
- Mention the result or impact of the project.

If you don't have an example that works or is hard to massage into a direct answer to this question, it will likely be hard to push your candidacy ahead and you may want to reconsider applying.

> **JerseyCoachAmy:** *If you have a skill, you have an example of using it. Period. Chances are even if you can skate by on an initial screen with a fluffed up semi-example here, you will get tripped up later in the process. Don't skimp on developing good examples of your skills.*

If you're presented with a question that does not seem to fall into one of these categories, refer to the "Tactics" section of Chapter 11 where you will find more in-depth advice for answering a multitude of question types.

Summary

- Always send a cover letter unless it explicitly states not to in the application process.
- Make it short and sweet, and put the focus on the value you can add in the position and your enthusiasm for joining the organization and industry. Craft an 80/20 cover letter template with the strongest selling points from your résumé highlighted, and some customization for the specifics mentioned above.
- Using templates will be a big help because you'll want to be able to respond quickly to an opportunity: speed, like enthusiasm, can make a big difference.
- Templates also allow you to increase the volume of résumés you send out for both networking and to apply for jobs. Job searching, like dating, is a numbers game. You increase your odds of finding what you are looking for every time you put yourself out there.
- Develop your own standard format for résumés and cover letters. You'll see mine in the examples, but you absolutely do not have to adopt mine. Use the font and spacing that you like, just be sure it doesn't crowd the page too much. Pull out your

dog-eared copy of Strunk & White's *Elements of Style* (do *not* tell me the one you got as a graduation gift is sitting in a box somewhere) or get a new one to make sure your style is grammatically correct. There's also a similar app for paring down language in the Hemingway style https://hemingwayapp.com/.

- Make sure your letter (wait for it . . . the Rule of Three is approaching) proves that you understand what the job is, that your experience will allow you to quickly add value in it, and that you have genuine enthusiasm for it. That Rule of Three only becomes more important the closer you get to an offer.

- Be prepared for additional questions to pop up when you log in to submit an official application with a final résumé and cover letter. You'll want to take some time to prepare answers for these, as they are important. Apply the general rules for résumés and cover letters in your answers: your answers should be honest, concise, and as specific to the job and organization as possible.

Next, we'll further condense the summaries you have created for your résumé and cover letter into an elevator pitch, and you'll learn how to use that elevator pitch to enhance your job applications with networking.

Chapter 7.
Develop Your Network

You now have the basic tools you need to apply for jobs. Hooray! This is usually where a lot of the guidance you are offered out there stops, but I want you to think of everything you just did as just a jumping-off point. You have the building blocks of what are going to be your more valuable tools, and those (surprise!) are the tools we are going to cover next: your elevator pitch and your network. Later, we'll put everything together into a cohesive job search strategy. Right now, let's focus on how and why it's important to develop a network. Does the phrase "networking" turn your stomach a little? That's fine. This chapter is for you too. Turns out your "network" is just the people you know. No big whoop.

Thinking of the people you know as your "network," a noun, may seem a little pompous. Your network is the web of people connected to you and to each other as friends, family, colleagues, and acquaintances. Call it whatever you want. Your network is not a foreign entity that runs parallel to your ordinary life and must be fed drinks after work while in a business suit. Your network is just the people you know, and the people your friends and acquaintances know. Period.

"Networking," the verb, is just staying in touch and on good terms with the people you know, as well as being open to meeting new people. Really, the only difference between just talking to people and networking is asking people for their contact information and permission to stay in touch. Asking someone if you can add them to your network can, indeed, sound a little pompous.[1] But asking someone if you can stay in touch is flattering. They know you may ask them for help someday, but they also know that someday you may be able to help them.

People who are great at networking, tend to just enjoy connecting people. In many companies, giving a referral for a candidate who gets hired means a cash bonus. There's every reason to talk to people about how they can help you and, a little farther down the road, how you can help each other. But if you ask for help in your job search, be sure to circle back with them and let them know how the connection panned out. They'll want to know where you wound up and to stay in touch. Someday, they'll want to put someone else in touch with you. You'll want to return the favor. Also, a cautionary note, you want to give as much support as you want to receive.

> **JerseyCoachAmy:** *If your version of networking is only finding and reaching out to people to help you when you are in need, you will suck at it. Touch base with people. Find out what's up. Recommend a book you enjoyed. If people know you're just calling to ask for something and you never give anything in return, you may as well go into telemarketing. No one is going to want to take your call.*

Here are some of the types of people already in your life that you can count as part of your network. I've personally been given major job search help from every type of person on this list or have had a client who has.

---

[1] If you're reading this LinkedIn, please change your standard invite language. Saying "I'd like to add you to my network" indicates "You have something I want." No thank you. I'd listen if the message was "Let's combine our networks. I think we both may benefit."

- Parents' friends, friends' parents, and the extended families of both
- Anyone you've ever met through school or an activity and almost everyone they know
- Medical providers, people with whom you or your friends walk dogs, and anyone who ever went to, sent a child to, or had a sibling spouse or parent go to one of your alma maters, including preschool and summer camp

It is entirely possible that someone to whom you reach out knows someone who happens to be looking for exactly what you are offering. This happens all the time. And the person with the professional need will be thrilled to hear of someone who may be able to meet their needs who comes with a personal recommendation or at least a personal connection.

If that's all a network is, why is networking such a big deal?

Your network is your most powerful asset because your network can help you get the inside track on a job or get your résumé noticed as the result of a personal endorsement. Your network can make the difference between getting an interview or not, getting a job offer or not. Your network can even make a difference in the quality and value of a job offer.

In this chapter we'll cover best practice tactics for turning your friends and acquaintances and everyone they know into your most powerful assets during your job search. First, we'll review exactly what networking goals you want to keep uppermost in your mind as you move forward because focusing on those simple goals helps make the process easier. Next, we'll create your best tool for this process: your elevator pitch. Then we'll talk about how to put your network to work for you, and how to specifically prepare for a networking meeting. Lastly, we'll review another key tool you'll need to create and maintain for both this process and for the overall job search: a database of contacts and network outreach.

Understanding Networking Goals

The goal of networking is to:

- Extract agreement that if you see an opening come up at this person's organization, they will forward your résumé and cover letter internally to the hiring manager or appropriate human resources representative.
- Extract names/organizations they can introduce you to, to do the same.
- Ask this person to keep you in mind for relevant positions they hear of at any organization, preferably before the job gets posted.

That's it. Always keep these goals in mind when you are looking for a job. Put yourself out there, and don't be surprised if help comes from unexpected places. The biggest favor someone can do for you is get you set up with as many people as possible to (1) make you aware of jobs that become available *before* they get posted, and / or (2) be willing to forward your résumé internally either before *or* after the role becomes available.

Your task is to quickly and cogently tee up for someone what you are looking for in your job search. You need enough focus to give people an idea of how they can help you, but not so much focus that they feel you are looking for something so specific they have nothing to offer. The elevator pitch is your best tool for presenting just the right level of detail to get people thinking about how they can help and who they may know.

In Chapter 3, we reviewed networking to learn how to talk to people about the work they do so you could understand more about working, and specifically what kind of work might be interesting to you. Your job was to make it easy for someone to explain his or her job to you and what that job means for the organization's customers, competitors, and overall market. This was to give you a better understanding of what you would be doing if you were to develop a similar career.

Now that you have a focus—either by industry (e.g., healthcare, green energy, software development) and/or function (e.g., research, sales, project management)—your networking goal is to find available jobs and get interviews. You now need to explain what you are looking for and how the person with whom you are talking could potentially help you.

Create Your Elevator Pitch

Remember people want to help *you*, but you need to help *them* by providing an easily digestible sound bite that gets them thinking about specific ways that they, or someone they know, may be able to help you. The elevator pitch is your sound bite. In the time it takes to complete an average elevator ride (approximately thirty to forty-five seconds) you need to be able to authentically walk through the three parts of the elevator pitch:

- "This is what I'm looking for."
- "Based on my experience and/or skills, this is why I know I'll be good at it."
- "Can you help me?"

That's all an elevator pitch is. You will need to be prepared to elaborate for a few more minutes if you get someone's attention. But it's those first few seconds that are key. You don't have much more time than that to (1) prove that you know what you want, (2) prove that you are genuine in your interest in learning from the other person, and (3) remember to ask for help.

JerseyCoachAmy: *If you don't ask, you don't get. Someone you know could know of someone who has a job that would be perfect for you.*

> *Even if you don't have a formal elevator pitch, you can start asking around. Get out from behind your computer! Jobs are not going to come looking for you.*

Let's talk about Don, who is interested in an entry-level sales role with a software company. Here are the fundamentals of his elevator pitch:

This Is What I'm Looking for:

- To add value to a sales organization with my strong work ethic and ability to develop relationships
- To leverage my excellent attention to detail that I've gained with years studying architecture, math, engineering, and other highly detailed disciplines
- To use my award-winning customer-service skills, gained from working customer-service roles part-time throughout high school and college

This Is How I Will Add Value:

- I'll be proactive about identifying what needs to get done and completing required tasks, often under tight time pressure.
    Examples:
    - Have a track record of working well in retail during high-pressure situations
    - Track record of teaching myself required technology skills, both proprietary and off the shelf, in school and professional settings
- I can juggle a number of demands at once.
    Examples:

- Got great GPA while always working at least twenty-eight hours per week
- Excelled in all work environments while also excelling at school
- I have the ability to create new methodologies and strategies to meet goals.

  Examples:
  - Created new processes for retail sales staff to meet and exceed sales goals
  - Generated sales at family construction company with new website interface and promotional campaigns on social media channels

This Is Why It Will Make Me Happy:

- I enjoy things that require hard work and discipline.
  - Running, learning new languages
- I'm creative.
  - Writing, cooking, exploring new media outlets, and watching social media evolve
- I'm adventurous.
  - Love travel and trying new things

Once you have created your own lists, you can create the foundation for your own elevator pitch. Here are some tips for translating your own lists:

- Look for themes: related things you have mentioned more than once.
- Ask what these themes say about you, for example,
  - adventurous or studious;
  - love people and working in teams, or like accomplishing things on your own;

- thrive under pressure, or get very anxious around deadlines;
- happiest when in front of a computer, or happiest out meeting people;
- love details, numbers, and analysis, or prefer developing relationships over power points and spreadsheets;
- enjoy making presentations and speaking in front of a group, or prefer to be behind the scenes.

• Ask yourself why you chose what you did to include in your list? What makes each appealing? Assign skill-related themes to the items on your list. Remember the three specific skills we discussed that are highly valued in any workplace setting? Here they are along with a few more. See if you recognize yourself in any of these characteristics below; be sure to cull out specific examples in this exercise.

- *Being detail oriented* so you don't make mistakes.
- *The ability to juggle multiple priorities at once* under time pressure while still paying attention to details.
- *Staying organized while juggling assigned tasks with efficiency and speed* so that when you complete them you can take on more.
- *Taking problems and breaking them down into action steps.* For example, knowing that you need to improve customer service is <u>interesting</u>, but knowing that what is needed for improvement is more rigorous training and better scripts is <u>important </u>for the customer-service reps.
- *Creative problem solving.* Every part of an organization—operations, strategy, finance, human resources, marketing—can benefit from creative employees who bring fresh energy and unique approaches to their daily tasks.
- *Link skills to experiences you have had*, even if they are not work experiences.

Let's go back to Don and see what this might look like:

- *The ability to juggle multiple priorities at once,* such as Don's ability to work an almost full-time job while also supporting his family's business and completing his degree
- *Efficiency and speed at completing assigned tasks,* such as being the kid who figured out how to change a bicycle chain before anyone else in his scout troop and as a result, had time to learn how to install a kickstand
- *Taking difficult things and breaking them down into simpler pieces,* such as understanding the reason why no one showed up at intramural lacrosse at 3:00 was because most of the players had lab until 4:15, so they needed to switch field times with intramural soccer
- *Creative problem solving,* such as figuring out how to get Don and his eight best college friends out of a bus station in Mexico where they have been stuck for twelve hours due to a ticket mix-up

Think about why you picked the things you did. Are there passions in your "real life" that are behind your choices? If they are genuine, they are appropriate to put into your analysis.

- Do you really want event planning because you love the feeling of being responsible for hundreds of details and pulling off something you thought could never be done?
- Do you want to do consumer-product goods marketing because you love going into beauty-product stores and checking out the new fragrances, colors, brands, and new formulae for shampoo?
- Do you love your volunteer work at a health clinic and want to be able to impact the policy under which the clinic runs?

Additional Considerations:

- Be specific about the *kind* of company where you would like to work, not necessarily the specific company where you want to work.
  - Bad: "I really want to work at Pepsi because they are on the cutting-edge of brand management."
  - Good: "I'm very interested in how brand management is changing as the result of social media and would love to work with consumer-packaged goods."

Why? Your target could lose interest quickly if they have no connection to Pepsi. This hurts you because that same person might know someone at Rubbermaid who hires entry level positions.

- Be specific about your skills, not necessarily how you would apply them.
  - Bad: "I really want to go into finance because I'm great at details and like working with numbers."
  - Good: "I'm great at keeping track of details and like working with numbers."

Why? Again, you don't want to limit the opportunities that could come your way. Your target could have an interesting idea about how financial modeling is being used within a human resource organization to forecast benefit expenses.

> **JerseyCoachAmy:** *Yes, a human resources department can need financial modeling from economics majors. And a logistics operation can need communication writers who were English majors. It's a thing. Don't think too literally.*

Develop three to five (never less than three and never more than five—it's a thing too[2]) bullet points in each of the following categories:

This Is What I'm Looking For:

Should answer the question "What do you want to do?"

This Is How I Will Add Value:

Should answer the question "What do you have to offer?"

Why This Will Make Me Happy:

Should answer the question "Why are you interested in this?"

Once you have grouped your answers to these three questions, you have the foundation of your elevator pitch. Once you have the foundation of your elevator pitch, you need to own it.

---

[2] I don't know why. When I was being trained as a consultant back at the dawn of time, they told us if you had more than three to five bullet points in a category you probably had two categories because that was too many bullet points and we had not broken down our points enough to be truly simple and powerful. This rule has served me well. Also, they told us we shouldn't use red markers on a white board when you are facilitating a group because red makes people angry. I don't know if that one is true, but I stick to blue and green anyway.

Element of Elevator Pitch	Should Answer the Question	Don's Example or Reason
This Is What I'm Looking for and Why It Would Make Me Happy	"What do you want to do? Why?"	"I'm very interested in joining a sales team where I can support new strategies and methodologies for getting and keeping customers. I've loved doing this for my family business and would love to support sales for a growing, collaborative tech business."
This Is How I Will Add Value:	"What do you have to offer?"	"I am a very hard worker and a quick learner. I am very customer-service focused, and my previous jobs have taught me what working under pressure and tight timelines is like. I've learned I really want to work with a tech product, as I know the teams tend to be more collaborative, and software is very interesting to me."
Can You Help Me?		"Can you help me?

You'll find a blank worksheet and more examples for developing your own elevator pitch in the accompanying or downloadable workbook (www.jobcoachamy.com/shop).

Additional Examples of an Elevator Pitch

- "I'm interested in learning about marketing consumer products—why do some companies decide to spend some money on digital ads and others spend money on free samples. I know I'm good at analyzing data so I could add value on the business side for a corporate team or agency. Can you help me? Do you know anyone in the field?
- "I like working with people and I don't like sitting behind a desk all day. A field that is based on building relationships seems like a good fit for me—maybe sales or some aspect of the real estate industry. Can you help me? Do you have any ideas?
- "I definitely like resolving tech issues, but I have no interest in being on a help desk or in a company's IT department. What I want to do is help build software or hardware products and make them better *before* they are in customer hands. Do you know of any roles like that? Can you help me?"

The key here is not to be judgmental about your interests or traits. You will save yourself countless hours of heartache if you admit now that you could not stand to be sitting behind a desk all day. Doing what you think you "should" do is rarely a formula for success.

Once you have a written elevator pitch, you need to own these words and get comfortable stringing them together in a way that is (a) authentic, and (b) easy to rattle off whenever you run into someone, anyone, who might be able to help. This means you are practicing

- in the shower,
- while you are exercising,

- with your pet,
- with your friends and family,

—and continuing until you are completely comfortable sharing your elevator pitch.

The bad news is this may be time-consuming. The good news is that your elevator pitch is going to be useful in all aspects of the job search process going forward.

If this exercise does not appeal as the means to finding the essence of what you want, find one that does. There are plenty of career tests out there that may be more scientific than what I've presented here and can give you more analytical results. Here are a few—costs range from free to under twenty dollars:

- Self-directed-search.org
- Mynextmove.org
- MyPlan.org
- Strengthsquest.com
- Assessment.com (MAPP Career Test)

Regardless of how you do it, narrow down your field of focus to something that you really *want*. This will be critical when interviewing because, as we'll review in the chapter on interviewing, the job most often goes to the candidate who wants the job the most. Presenting yourself authentically for a role you both understand and want is what is going to make you the most attractive to a hiring manager. Skipping this step will ultimately impact your candidacy overall. Even if you get the job, you can be the one who suffers in the long run. Now is the time to be accountable to yourself for what you spend forty-plus hours a week doing. As the saying goes, "If you don't know where you want to go, you'll wind up someplace else."

> **JerseyCoachAmy:** *If you can't get across quickly what you want in a job and why, go home and stay there until you can.*

> **JerseyCoachAmy:** *The more you talk to people, the more you increase your chances of finding out about jobs that are, or are becoming, available. Period. You want a job in sales but don't think it's worth telling the nurse giving you a flu shot? That nurse likely has four business cards of salespeople wanting to sell her stuff lying around on her desk. Tell her! She may let you take a photo of them and use her name.*

Examples are Really, Really Important

Telling me you are hardworking is nice. Giving me an example and adding that you have had two jobs since you were a sophomore in high school is powerful. Unless you have an example, you are only giving me adjectives.

If you tell me on your resume that you have excellent verbal and communication skills, tell me what you have in your background that allows you to make that claim. You can't just tell me what you think I want to hear. I want to know thoughtful reasons, hear about specific experiences, or see written examples.

We'll go into greater depth and specifics on this in Chapter 11 as you prepare for interviews. At this stage of the job search process, you still want to be able to back up a statement with an example. Consider the difference between job seekers Max, Ned, and Steve below. They are networking with Eric, an executive at Corrugated Rubber Industries, and hoping to be recommended for an entry-level role there.

ERIC: "Why do you want to work for Corrugated Rubber Industries?"

MAX: "...it would be cool."

This tells Eric that Max did not do his homework, is just saying what he (Eric) "wants to hear," and may have no idea what Corrugated Rubber Industries does. Even if Eric were Max's godfather, he may find it difficult to recommend Max internally.

ERIC: "Why do you want to work for Corrugated Rubber Industries?"

NED: "The materials you use are sustainable, which fits my values. You have also been growing quickly and adding so many more offices that I hope one day I may be able to get an overseas assignment."

This tells Eric that Ned did do his homework and has put thought into a potential career with the company. Eric would be more likely to recommend Ned, who will likely reflect a genuine interest in the role and make Eric look pretty good. However, Ned has only talked about how the company is a fit for him. He has not talked at all about how he could be a fit for the company.

ERIC: "Why do you want to work for Corrugated Rubber Industries?"

STEVE: "I want to be in an organization that is very fast-paced, and I know that because your packaging materials are sustainable, you are growing very quickly. I worked on the campus television station, and we were always scrambling to get our shows on the air on time and with the correct information, and I loved how fast everything moved. I also have very good grades in accounting, finance, and economics, so I know that I can add value in this role in the treasury department. This is a job where I can add value, learn a lot, and be happy every day because things move fast."

This is likely the candidate that Eric would recommend with the greatest confidence. Steve is the person who used examples not only to explain why he wanted to work at the company, but also used examples to explain why he knew he would both add value and enjoy the work.

Here are a few other people who approach Eric for networking purposes. They are not interviewing for the role, but Eric is chatting with them at an alumni career fair:

MOLLIE: "I'm really interested in web design and starting a career where I can put the skills I've learned in school to use with a company that does web design for clients. I've got a good mix of technical and creative, which is what I enjoy and am good at doing. Do you know anybody who works in a company like this?"

This is a good pitch because even though it is not what Eric does, he may have a best friend that runs a company just like this that he would be happy to reach out to on Mollie's behalf.

Katie takes a different and somewhat more open-ended approach:

"My interest, all through school and in the internships I've had, has been in website design. Linking the creative and the technical is really interesting to me. Do you have an internal department at Corrugated Rubber Industries that may be hiring an entry-level role, or do you know of anyone who hires this kind of position?"

Bevin's elevator pitch is less open-ended and will narrow down the chances of Eric being able to help her significantly:

"I want a web design career with Digitas in either their New York or Paris offices. I know I can add value, as I've done work on my own and in school on designing websites, and I'd love to design websites for Digitas's corporate clients."

By the way, Don (real client, fake name) got into the Customer Success department of a rapidly growing data security enterprise software firm and loves his job. In fact, he is running his own team now. Customer Success doesn't sell the software but supports customers after they have bought it—helping to solve problems as they arise, provide information on additional modules and upgrades as they may become available, and generally keeping the relationship good. He loves his job.

And our friend Elaine (also real client, fake name) got a job as a media planner working for one of the largest digital publishers serving the Spanish-speaking community in New York. This means she worked matching the available inventory of ad space "pages" to the advertisers who wanted to place their digital branding and promotional campaigns on those pages. She worked closely with (1) the account executives whose clients were the advertisers, (2) the publishers who identified, priced, and created the inventory of available space to be sold to the advertisers, and (3) the technology team that published the content. Once ads were matched to spaces, she worked with the tech team to make sure the ads showed up in the right places at the right times. She did not love the work, though, and after about eighteen months, she went back to graduate school for another degree in Spanish and is loving teaching.

Mobilize Your Network for a General Search

What you want to do now is use your elevator pitch to find people with whom you can set up phone calls, video call, coffee meetings, or short informational interviews to get your story out. Start with your network. Mention that you're in a job search and give your elevator pitch or send an email. Here's an example of a general networking email:

Hi Courtney,

I am a fellow UVA soon-to-be alumnus in the Marketing Analytics program, graduating this spring. I noticed on LinkedIn that you also have a degree in marketing and have gone down an interesting career path from Mullen to Design Interactive. I am very interested in both companies and was hoping you could share with me your experience working there as well as your transition from UVA to where you are now. I appreciate your time and hope to hear from you soon.

Best,

Aaron

You can also send a LinkedIn request, but if you do, always add something personal: the generic text is too easy to throw out or ignore. Remember to ask for time, ideas, contact names and information, and research ideas. If a mutual friend made you aware of Courtney, add that to the letter: "I learned about your career and our UVA connection through our mutual friend at the city swimming pool, Lisa Block." Don't be shy about pursuing any possible lead through any possible connection. What is the worst that can happen? The person thinks "Ugh, I feel badly but I don't have time" and deletes the email. What's the best that could happen? They are looking for someone just like you to fill a role, or just had lunch with someone who did. When in doubt, reach out.

> If Aunt Migs gave you her college roommate's daughter Clare's contact information insisting that she is a bigwig at a technology company, but it turns out she is in purchasing at a shipping company—still have the call! You never know.

Cast a wide net and include your alumni databases, camp friends, and distant cousins. Attach your résumé or a link to your LinkedIn profile if given permission, or offer to send it in your follow-up correspondence along with a cover email that can be forwarded to a relevant contact so that all the person in your network has to do is hit "forward."

Making it as easy as possible for the person on the receiving end of your request to help you is key. For example, if you recently met Hunter at a get-together and he is working at Wayfair, where you too would like to work, and you asked him if he would be willing to send in your résumé internally if something became available, and he agreed—you *don't* want to send him just this email:

EMAIL #1

Re: recent job posting

Dear Hunter,

We spoke a few weeks ago about my interest in Wayfair when we met at Sawyer's barbecue. Recently a role became available as a copywriter at Wayfair, and I am hoping that you may be able to forward my résumé internally, as we discussed. I have also applied online through regular channels, but I know that having my résumé additionally come through an internal source will improve my chances. Thank you so much in advance.

Kind regards,

Maddy

If Maddy sends that email, Hunter is going to need to think about who needs to see that and what he should say when he sends it on.

What would be much better for you and much easier for him, would be if you send the email above but add in this line at the end:

"I will send you a second, separate email with a cover letter that you can forward shortly.

When you send this email, then all Hunter needs to do is hit one button to help you out in a big way.

EMAIL #2

Re: Copywriter Position, ID Code CW_632

Dear Hunter,

Thank you in advance for forwarding my résumé and cover letter (attached) for consideration for the above-referenced position at Wayfair. I am extremely enthusiastic about the opportunity and appreciative of your support. As you will see from the attached, my qualifications include:

- Several years of on- and off-campus copywriting roles
- Demonstrated work ethic and a strong GPA (3.1), leadership in campus publications, and 20-hour/week part-time job throughout college
- Willingness to learn and great fan of Wayfair!

With thanks,

Maddy

Attachments

If you don't hear back, follow up with another email, text, or phone call in about a week. Then let it go. Not everyone will make networking a priority to get back to you, and that is *fine*. At every stage of the job search now, volume is key because the more you put out there (requests for information, job applications, networking invitations, etc.) the higher your odds are that someone will respond.

When you are referred a name and contact of someone you don't know but who has the potential to be really helpful, send an email directly. This will have more of an impact than a LinkedIn request, which is easier to ignore. Put the name of the person that suggested you talk in the subject line of the email so they won't toss your request into junk mail. Ask if you can schedule a short call—suggest commuting time or anything that might be convenient for them. Maybe offer to treat them to a coffee or a beer. Use your elevator pitch.

Here is a sample email for contacting someone you don't know:

Re: Referral from Hudson Linsky

Dear Mr. Cassidy,

My neighbor, Hudson Linsky, suggested that I reach out to you as I am currently seeking to learn all I can about construction management. I have just finished my first year of professional work after college as a Property Administrator for Commercial Realty Associates. I have learned a great deal and am lucky to have had the opportunity to grow my administration and client management skills significantly. At this point I am considering my next challenge and am very interested in pursuing something that is faster-paced and more challenging.

I have a strong work ethic and enjoy taking the initiative to make sure jobs are completed well, on time, and to the satisfaction of all involved. You will see from the attached résumé that I bring to my work:

- Customer service focus and attention to detail
- Ability to quickly learn processes and tasks
- Track record of strong work product and building good internal and external client relationships

It would be a privilege to speak with you to learn more about your career path, your company, and your industry. I would also be very interested in knowing if my skills may be applicable to any roles you may need to fill in the near future. If we could speak for a few minutes by phone or Zoom, or if I may come to your office for a short informational interview, I would be very appreciative. I hope to hear from you.

Kind regards,

Megan St. John
Résumé Attached

JerseyCoachAmy: *Almost everyone loves to talk about themselves. When you reach out to someone, listen to what they have to say. The more fascinated you are, the greater the chances they will want to help you. Is this a cynical strategy? Sure. Is this a successful strategy? You bet.*

Be bold. Most people enjoy hearing from someone who is interested in their work. When you've asked everyone you know personally for recommendations, turn to your alumni database to see if you can email anyone who works in an industry or function that you are targeting. Move on to friends of friends and their extended family. You never know. Be creative. Be comprehensive. Don't be discouraged, and if you find yourself discouraged, then go ahead and take a break for a few days. Cast a wide net and expect a few responses that will lead to more.

At any stage of your career, one of your most valuable tools can be your alumni database or the software (as of this writing, Handshake is the one used most often) that allows you to find and contact someone who shares part of your history. You can search by job function, industry, city/state/country, or level. Your chances of getting someone to return an email are higher with a personal connection of some sort.

Mobilize Your Network for a Specific Opportunity

Once you learn of an available opportunity and want to give yourself a better shot at it, use the methods above to find an internal employee, or a close friend or former colleague of one. Additionally, ask friends and family to go on LinkedIn and see if their networks turn up anyone at the company; LinkedIn is great at serving up people by organization. Your alumni database should also be searchable by company name.

Here's what to do if you are lucky enough to hit pay dirt:

- Get the relevant contact's email address. If you can only get a name, you can usually figure out the organization's email convention by perusing the "contact us" section of the company website.
- Put the name of your contact or school in the email header so it makes it through whatever spam filters may be in place. Remember! You'll need to ask permission from the person who gave you the contact to use their name.
- Attach the file that you submitted formally: résumé and cover letter with file named for the convenience of the internal team Your Name Position Title as mentioned previously. If relevant, add any other items that were requested in application, such as a writing sample.
- Write an email that leads with how you know the contact (or mentions your shared love of your alma mater, or the like).
- State that you've applied for the job and have attached your application to this email.
- Ask the contact to forward your information internally to the appropriate person.
- Ask if you may follow up with them for a potential informational interview.

Make forwarding your résumé as easy as possible for them by making the email one that they can forward exactly as is.

JerseyCoachAmy: *This doesn't always work, but it always increases your chances.*
And that's what we're going for.

After completing these steps, make sure to follow the preparation reviewed above for general networking by familiarizing yourself with the individual's background and organization. That way, should they happen to call you back quickly, you'll be able to have an intelligent conversation.

If you have not heard back from this contact for a week, draft a gentle email asking if your email was received and if it would be possible to discuss the role and your candidacy. If you don't hear back after that, let it go. The individual may be too busy or may know that the position has already been filled. Don't circle back to your original contact, if there is one, to complain. Remember only this: the lack of response is not about you or your candidacy.

Having said that, do not be shy about reaching out. As mentioned previously, many companies offer bonuses to employees who identify new hires, so you may be offering your contact a chance at a bit of extra income.

Email Sleuthing: Sometimes you can find a person you want to contact, but not their email. To find a company's email, put the search terms "email conventions for *company name*" into your search engine. Most times, it will immediately return a short paragraph that indicates the most common convention and the percentage of time it is used at the company. Occasionally, you'll need to make two or three attempts before you'll find the right email address. If you don't get it right, it will just bounce back, so no harm, no foul. Other ways to identify the correct email convention include looking on the company website, which will often list emails for the company leaders. If not, you can sometimes find a direct email for the investor relations professional on the page that has press releases and deduce an appropriate email for your would-be connection from that.

Remember to put your connection to the person—name, college name, etc.—in the subject line of the email or it may go to a junk mail file.

Prepare for Your Networking Meeting

Once you've scheduled a meeting or call, spend some time preparing to make the most of the valuable time you have been given. First, take a look at the individual's online profile. See if you can understand what the individual does and how their job may relate to your own goals.

Next, develop some educated questions based on the research you do on their company's website. Never assume that you have their job all figured out, just aim for a broad understanding. All companies work differently and have different nomenclature for departments.

In order to go into the meeting well prepared, go back to the exercises we used for soft networking or networking to learn about what jobs there are:

- Identify the company's market.

- American Airlines (AA), for example, is in the travel market and makes its money bringing people to various destinations on their airplanes.
- Identify the company's customer.
  - AA's customers are travelers: business, leisure, economy, luxury, family—anyone who wants to fly somewhere that AA does.
- Identify the company's competition.
  - AA's competition is other airlines: domestic, such as United; regional, like SkyWest; and international, such as British Airways. Basically, any airline that shares the same route, and in some cases, other forms of transportation such as rail or ship.

If you know these three things about a company, it becomes much easier to have an interesting and educated discussion. If you have a contact that is in purchasing, for example, you know they are getting the elements that keep the company running. They may be buying plane fuel or contracting food services for flights or the paper products for the airline's planes and offices or maybe even the uniforms the crew wear. These are good, informed questions to ask.

Marketing people would be focused, overall, on getting customers to fly American over other carriers, which may mean advertising in-flight entertainment ("We have fewer boring flights!") or creating competitive mileage-rewards programs ("We'll reward you for your loyalty to us!").

Human resources staff would be focused on keeping the pilots, ground crew, flight attendants, and gate personnel happy. Or a more sophisticated role could be ensuring that the company understands and complies with the employment laws and practices in all the different countries in which the airline operates.

We'll go through how to analyze a company and a job description in much greater depth in Chapter 10 as you move on to preparing for interviews. At this point, any kind of question that indicates you made an effort to understand what the individual and their company is about will go a long way.

Remember, however, the best questions are the ones whose answers you want to know.

JerseyCoachAmy: *People love talking about themselves—to a point. Don't be an idiot and ask why someone left a job or an industry. If the company has been making headlines, don't bring it up. (All their relatives already have.) You are trying to build good rapport with them before you ask if they would help you out, not alienate them.*

Good question: "What about your industry makes it interesting to you?"

Bad question: "You don't look at all like your LinkedIn picture. How old is that photo?"

Bad idea question (e.g., "I want to prove how smart I am"): "I read in the news you just canceled an order for new planes and your stock is tanking. What's up with that?"

Unlike normal interviewing sessions, because *you* requested the meeting, you should ask your questions first and only talk about your own background when invited to do so.

A good place to start the interview is to ask the individual to tell you their story.

- How did they get started in the professional world?
- What advice would they give you? What was the best advice they ever got?
- What is it they actually do in their current role? What skills make them successful in that role?

- Are there others they think might be willing to speak with you about roles in their organizations?

Keep an eye on the time. When you get to the point in the conversation where there is only five minutes left, mention that time is almost up. If the person offers to continue a little longer, great! They will appreciate it either way if they know you respect their time.

Tell your story when asked. Get across key points but use your time wisely to *be sure* to define next steps before you close.

Key Points for the Network Call

- Would your contact be willing to recommend you for a role if one becomes available at their organization? Forward your résumé internally? Forward your résumé to other organizations/individuals that/whom they know well? Which ones?
- What can you provide in order to make this as easy as possible for them? Draft an email that they can send? Send an email yourself but use their name?
- Ask yourself what other points that you discussed require follow up?
  - If another person was mentioned, is that someone they recommend you speak with? If so, what is the easiest way to follow up? Would it be okay to send a follow-up email requesting that person's contact information, or can you take the contact information now (over the phone, or Zoom, or via text)?
  - Was another company mentioned? Do they know of someone at that company who could be a resource? Could you reach out and use their name as a connection?
  - Are there any publicly available resources such as blogs, conference papers, or industry association sites your contact cited? Ask for the details.

Before the meeting ends, ask for ideas or recommendations about your job search generally. Ask for specifics: names, companies, recommended blog or book titles, other people with whom you can speak, etc. You want to be able to end each call with a few action items.

> **JerseyCoachAmy:** *If your contact can't think of anyone else or anything else that can be helpful to you, ask if you can email back in a week after they have thought about it. It's a graceful way to not let them off the hook entirely and give them one more chance. They might not reply to the follow up email, but they also might. It's worth a shot.*

Close with appreciation and reiterate the next steps so they know what to expect from you. Promptly send a quick thank you by email, and a handwritten note later.

Tips:

- Be yourself and enjoy the conversation. This is someone you'd like to have in your network long-term.
- The conversation should flow, so do not worry about following the structure I've laid out exactly.
- It is okay to let the person with whom you are speaking know that you have a list of questions/issues in front of you to make sure you cover everything. They will be happy you did some preparation.
- Take notes and use them in subsequent discussions about this role or others like this one.
- Keep a watch handy to make sure that you are staying within the defined time; start the wrap-up five minutes before the time the person indicated they need to stop.

- Send a handwritten thank-you note, if possible. A note will be more memorable than an email and will stand out as a gesture of gratitude on its own if you are also sending follow-up emails. Think about a way to offer something of value as a thank you too:
  - A book, blog, or TED talk relevant to an issue you discussed that the person may find interesting
  - News about your shared connection, maybe the professor you both had or the friend you both know
  - A recommendation for a shared hobby or interest you found, e.g. interesting places to fish

You'll find a worksheet with examples on how to structure a networking call in the accompanying workbook.

Create and Maintain a Database of Contacts

Start a spreadsheet or document with the following information so you don't get confused about whom you contacted at what company and when you need to follow up:

Name	Title	Company	Contact Info

Date Contacted	Summary of Discussion	Follow-Up Date	Notes

Include EVERYTHING and EVERYBODY. Today's complete dead end can become next month's hot lead.

You'll find a blank contact database worksheet in the accompanying workbook.

Keep track of the discussions in whatever format works best for you. Most of my clients prefer using Excel or Word, but there are far more sophisticated products on the market as well. Paper works, too, if you want to purchase a notebook and keep your details there.

As mentioned above, be sure to circle back with everyone on this list once you accept a position. Very few people do this, so circling back can really make you stand out.

Example:

- Interested in healthcare marketing? Start asking friends if they know anyone who works in the field.
- Great news! Your neighbor's sister is head of marketing for a hospital system. Will your neighbor ask if her sister will talk to you for a few minutes about the field? If so, when is the next time your neighbor will talk to her sister?
- Okay, if they are going to talk next week, then you will circle back in a week to find out what she said.

Name	Title	Company	Contact Info
Julie	Neighbor	N/A	555-555-1111

Date Contacted	Summary of Discussion	Follow-Up Date	Notes
5/7	Daughter Katie heads hospital marketing and may talk to me about healthcare marketing.	5/14	Ask Julie about it again in a week; will have talked to Katie by then.

Name	Title	Company	Contact Info
Katie	SVP, Marketing	Northern Virginia Hospital System	

Date Contacted	Summary of Discussion	Follow-Up Date	Notes
			Waiting for more info from Julie on 5/14.

Notes:

- Don't leave things open-ended. Ask how much time the person needs to contact their friend (or family member, or colleague, etc.), then say that you will follow up with them after that amount of time has passed. For example, "If you're going to talk to your aunt on Sunday about whether her law firm is hiring interns, I'll send you an email on Monday to follow up, okay?"
- Record the interaction in your database to remind yourself when and how you agreed to get in touch. You should be initiating a lot of these kinds of networking opportunities every week, so you will want to keep track of the details so they don't become confusing.

JerseyCoachAmy: *This record keeping is important and easy to do. I guarantee you will regret it if you do not keep some form of record with the names, dates, and companies you contacted during your search. You will go back to it more than once and for years in the future. I kid you not.*

Summary

- Your "network" is just the people you know.
- Networking is just talking to people about what they do and what you want to do. It's also about asking permission to stay in touch in case you can ever help each other out. In that way, these people become part of your "network."
- Most people are interested in meeting new people for these purposes, so you shouldn't feel shy.
- Use your elevator pitch to explain what you do and what your skills are, and then get people talking about themselves.
- Keep a record of the people you know professionally, or just meet in a job search. Include when, how, and where you met. Check in with them from time to time in a professional way. Pay it forward by letting them know if you can help them out.
- If you are actively job searching, the goal of networking has three (you're gobsmacked, right?!) additional objectives:
  - To see if you can learn about jobs before they are posted
  - To ask your contact if they will (before or after a job is posted) forward your application (i.e., résumé and cover letter) internally
  - To ask your contact about friends in other organizations you could reach out to who may consider doing the same thing for you
- If you know someone well who works at a company where you are applying, ask him or her to also act as an inside reference for you. If you know more than one, ask them all.
- Every time you contact someone for professional purposes, you should begin with expressing appreciation for the person's time. End with asking permission to be in touch with them again if, for example, a position of interest becomes available within their organization.

- Professional contacts, like friendships, need tending over time. Don't only be in touch when you need something. Return calls and emails. Pay it forward when people reach out to you for help. Reach out when you don't need anything and check in. I'm not recommending doing anything that feels inauthentic—but if a contact comes to mind when you run into a mutual friend or some such connection, consider sending a quick email or text. Maybe forward a particularly interesting TED talk. It's a nice thing to do, and people appreciate it. It will help your network grow and become more valuable.

Next, we'll review how to put all your tools together into an effective, four-part job search structure. You'll use your tools in this structure: résumé, cover letter, elevator pitch, and networking skills. By setting weekly accountability goals in multiple job search areas, you will really start working this process. In the next chapter we'll review how.

Chapter 8.
Develop a Job Search Structure

There's no getting around it: job searching is a job. You'll need to commit time and effort to it, and you'll need all the tools we've developed for you so far: your résumé, cover letter, elevator pitch, and networking plans. Combining these tools with a comprehensive job search structure will allow you to set, accomplish, and track interim goals along the way to finding a new position.

Why is it important to have a structure and interim goals?

- You can't job search twenty-four hours a day. You will make yourself crazy and stop making progress somewhere around the time you start researching exes and what your grade-school teachers are doing now between applications.
- You're not going to find a job right away. Finding a job takes time. I tell most of my clients to plan for an average of four to six months, but certainly the process can be as little as a month or as much as a year depending on your skill base, how specific your parameters are, and how hard you are willing to work on your search. There are a lot of random and unpredictable factors that can range from a CFO being out of the country for two weeks and thus unable to sign off on a new hire, to a human resources coordinator inadvertently misplacing the interviewers' comments

about all the candidates for your role and then went out of office, so now, no one else can find them and the whole process gets set back a week. In either of these scenarios: (1) you would never know what happened and the company would be loath to admit it, and (2) it could stretch out the cycle of feedback for you from days to weeks or even months. Both scenarios may be equally likely to result in your getting the job, albeit delayed, the job going to someone else, or the job getting eliminated in the budgeting process after being open for so long that someone decides the position just isn't necessary after all. The key thing to remember is that these factors have nothing to do with your skills, how well you did in the interview, or (and really, really remember this) your chances of getting *another* job.

Having weekly goals allows you the peace of mind to know that you've done all that you can reasonably do to advance your goal of becoming employed. When the end of the week comes, you can relax without guilt. Because, even if you did not find your next job, at least you achieved the goals you set for yourself. A job search, by definition, is most often out of your own control, but you can control how hard you work at the goals you set.

The Track Structure

There are multiple kinds of activities required in the job search. A comprehensive structure will allow you to track all of them in an organized system. I recommend conducting a job search in at least three tracks, and potentially up to five depending on your stage of life and current employment status. For each, set a weekly goal for yourself. Stick to it, and ask someone in your life to help hold you accountable to your goals so that you can't blow them off.

Here is an overview of my comprehensive five-track approach, followed by a more complete description of each track individually.

	Name	Description	Effort	Impact
Track 1	REACTIVE	Apply to jobs already posted.	Easiest	Least Effective
Track 2	PROACTIVE	Network to try and find jobs before they are posted.	Hardest	Most Effective
Track 3	PROFESSIONAL DEVELOPMENT	Find blogs, journals, websites, case studies, LinkedIn groups, and other ways to read up on your area of interest.	Should be fun, or you've chosen the wrong area of interest.	Everything you learn will be useful at some point— maybe what will make you stand out in your next interview. Keep note of what you learn.
Track 4	STAY BUSY	You need a project to prove you are high-energy if you are out of work more than one month.	Can be a few hours a month to a few days a week.	Provides a solid answer to the question "What have you been doing?"

	Name	Description	Effort	Impact
Track 5	TAKE ADVANTAGE OF YOUR TIME	Use your time to do something for yourself that you couldn't do if you were working.	As much or little as you want.	Shows confidence. Makes you interesting. You'll never regret it.

The following is a more detailed description of each of these five tracks in sequence.

Track 1: Reactive

	Name	Description	Effort	Impact
Track 1	REACTIVE	Apply to jobs already posted.	Easiest	Least Effective

- Subscribe to job alerts from the organizations you have identified as ones where you would really enjoy working.
- Sign up for Indeed alerts using key words (e.g., marketing, entry level, consumer products, agency, etc.); for nonprofit work, try Idealist. LinkedIn also has good job postings. Also, you can just type in your key words, "jobs," and a location into Google to find additional job boards that are relevant for your geographic area and area of interest.
- Set a goal of how many jobs you will seek to apply to each week. Go for three to eight, weekly, for best results.
- Keep the pipeline full even if you are in the process at one or two firms that seem promising. You never know.
- Don't expect to hear back from many of the jobs where you apply,

if any of them. It's a numbers game: you increase your odds of getting a call the more you apply.

- Don't get mad or take it personally if you don't hear back. Recruiters and HR teams are often overwhelmed and under-staffed. Everyone is sincerely trying to do the best they can with limited resources. You may have very impressive qualifications, but there may be five other résumés that came in ahead of yours who did the exact same job at a competitor. Or there may be an application from the CEO's nephew or the son of the CEO of the company's biggest customer. You may never know, but suffice it to say this does not happen because you suck, or due to any of the other reasons that will flood your brain when you are trying to sleep at night.

- Other reasons why you may not hear back that have nothing to do with your candidacy:

  - Legally, jobs must be posted briefly even if an internal candidate has already been identified. Check to see if the posting disappears quickly.

  - Sometimes postings are not as fresh as declared online—you may have applied when an offer has already been extended to another candidate.

  - The sheer volume of résumés received means it's a lot of work to send out the "thanks, but no thanks" emails if the process is not automated, and no process is 100 percent foolproof.

- Don't be discouraged. Plenty of people actually do apply for jobs online cold and get them. It happens. It could happen to you.

- After you've applied:

  - Follow up with networking research: Do you know anyone who works there? Does anyone you know have a contact there? If you can get your résumé passed on to the hiring manager internally or to the recruiter on the posting, you significantly increase your chances of getting a call. (For more detailed instructions, see Chapter 7, Networking for a Specific Opportunity.)

Track 2: Proactive

	Name	Description	Effort	Impact
Track 2	PROACTIVE	Network to try and find jobs before they are posted.	Hardest	Most Effective

JerseyCoachAmy: *There are plenty of ways to find people to talk to on your own and add people to your network. This is all about using networking tools to get a jump on the competition.*

Here are a few specific recommendations for this aspect of your job search:

- Focus on up to three industries or roles (e.g., entry-level marketing position in an agency that works with consumer products or a consumer products company).
- Identify ten to fifteen companies on which to focus.
  - Follow them on LinkedIn and Twitter. I once had a client whose résumé was selected over several hundred others because the CEO cross-referenced those who had applied with those who had liked a recent article he published on LinkedIn.
  - For each company, gain an understanding of how they make money, who their customer is, and who their competitors are.

- Look on GlassDoor to find out what you can about their entry-level roles and ensure the pay level meets your needs.
- Identify key clients, campaigns, programs, or products (particularly, "what's new" and what makes them proud right now).
- Look for books and articles related to each organization's work.

These tips will help when you're working to identify potential contacts:

- As mentioned earlier, you can identify alumni contacts by getting a username and password for your college's alumni office and search by relevant key terms.
- Identify network contacts on LinkedIn who might be helpful and reach out to them; create a custom message that references how you know the person and that you would like to follow them professionally.[1]
- If you are targeting a specific company, you can search LinkedIn by typing in the name of the company and the key words "Talent Acquisition" to see if a name appears that seems relevant to the area or role you are seeking and reach out to that person directly. Try finding the company's email convention first (see Chapter 7. Develop Your Network), but if all else fails, try to make a connection through LinkedIn.
- Set a goal for yourself. For example, identify and reach out to five contacts per week.

---

[1] Overall, LinkedIn is great at teeing up a list of people you may know. Check out their section for you on this regularly and use it.

> **JerseyCoachAmy:** *Don't be afraid to put yourself out there. This part can be tough at first but it's also really rewarding. Connect with your own inner-Jersey.*

Track 3: Professional Development

	Name	Description	Effort	Impact
Track 3	PROFESSIONAL DEVELOPMENT	Find blogs, journals, websites, case studies, LinkedIn groups, and other ways to read up on your area of interest.	Should be fun, or you've chosen the wrong area of interest.	Everything you learn will be useful at some point— maybe what will make you stand out in your next interview. Keep note of what you learn.

- Spend some time each week reading up on your industry and companies of choice.
- Join free professional associations.
- Read the leading blogs in your field.
- Follow appropriate LinkedIn groups and experts. Read what they publish.
- See if there are podcasts, documentaries, or books that relate to your field.
- Spend some time with general interest podcasts, documentaries, or books to keep your mind sharp. There is a lot of really

interesting content available to read, watch, and listen to. Look until you find something that is of interest to you. One idea is to pick one thing that is related to your career and one thing that is not.

You never know what is going to come up in an interview: something that was published in *Harvard Business Review's* Tip of the Day or an article you read in *Outdoors*. Stay engaged and inspired, and keep note of what you learn about your field of interest and any ideas or questions that occur to you. You never know what may be valuable later on.

> Vary your goals based on your schedule: less time during busy weeks, more time during slow ones. Always try to allow some time for all three tracks however, but if you only have time for one, focus on Track 2.

Track 4: Stay Busy

	Name	Description	Effort	Impact
Track 4	STAY BUSY	You need a project to prove you are high-energy if you are out of work more than one month.	Can be a few hours a month to a few days a week.	Provides a solid answer to the question "What have you been doing?"

If you are out of school or out of work, you need to add another project or activity to your weekly schedule. The benefits of doing this accrue for you:

- *As a candidate:* almost every employer wants someone who is a "go-getter" and motivated to make a difference. Finding a way to become involved and add value of your own without anyone telling you how, where, or when, can make you a highly valued employee. Someone who is happy to sit around and nap until the next thing comes along is not necessarily going to be the person a hiring manager wants on the team—they could be more likely to sit around and nap unless you are telling them, every minute, what to do and how.
- *As an individual:* doing things for other people, having a routine, and waking up every day with a purpose will make you feel good. Job searching can be lonely, hard, and draining. Your tendency may be to want to shut yourself off from family and friends until you have landed that next role. Don't fall into that trap. Taking on a project will help protect you from yourself.

Contact local community groups with which you may have an affiliation or interest and think about how your skills might be of service to them, then talk to them and find out what they need. It could be a church, school, or local nonprofit. State upfront that you are not sure when you might be starting a job on sudden notice, but that you would be happy to help with something while you have time. Idealist.org is a great place to start looking for formal volunteer opportunities in your town.

Project examples:

- Record books for the blind
- Improve the website or database at a small community service organization

- Join a fundraiser or fundraising event team at a local school
- Decide to start a blog or publish your thoughts on a particular subject on LinkedIn
- Do that family history project that you've been wanting to do for years

All of these projects: require you to get out of your head, show that you have the motivation to push yourself, and require you to use some skills. Projects can be broad-based or narrow and may serve your entire community or just your family.

> **JerseyCoachAmy:** *What matters is that you set a goal, stay accountable, and achieve something. C'mon! Get off the freakin' couch.*

Track 5: Personal Time Investments

	Name	Description	Effort	Impact
Track 5	TAKE ADVANTAGE OF YOUR TIME	Use your time to do something for yourself that you couldn't do if you were working.	As much or little as you want.	Shows confidence. Makes you interesting. You'll never regret it.

It is awful to be at loose ends without a paycheck, but as soon as you have a paycheck, it will be awful to think that you had the time to get certified in Reiki, or learn to windsurf, or master the art of making sourdough bread—and you did not. You're allowed to do something that makes you happy. Learn to play harmonica. Get in shape. Read the Federalist Papers. Remember, Interest-*ED* is interest-*ING*? This counts. With a library card and an adventurous spirit, there are interesting projects to be had at any budget level.

You'll find a Weekly Goal Worksheet with examples in the accompanying or downloadable workbook (www.jobcoachamy.com/shop).

Unexpected Benefits

You may find unexpected benefits to Tracks 4 and 5 in the form of new contacts, new ideas, and evolving considerations for your search. Taking the time to expand your circles, your activities, and your lens on the world can lead to extraordinary results. Pick what feels right for you and watch what happens.

Again, the Importance of Record Keeping

We talked about the importance of record keeping in Chapter 4 on Networking, but it's worth mentioning again because your job search is likely to outlast your memory for details. Keep a record of when, how, and why you contacted someone during the course of your job search, as well as the outcome of those conversations. A spreadsheet with the name, organization, contact info, date of contact, and follow-up of everyone to whom you reach out will do the trick.

A few more important reasons for being diligent:

- Your neighbor's cousin, who was of absolutely no help last week, may become the hiring manager of a killer opportunity in three months.
- This won't be the only job search of your career; you can use this as a starting place for your next one too. Two or three years from now, guaranteed (I'm not kidding—I know this—trust me), you are going to run into one of these people and not be able to place

them. You may be interviewing one of them to work for you, or they may be interviewing you for something else. Seems weird, but you would be surprised at how often this happens.

JerseyCoachAmy: *I have kind of a freakish memory for stuff that does not matter. It's a blessing and a curse. No one likes hanging out with me at reunions because I remember all the other people their spouses slept with before they got married. Anyway, once I was interviewing people at an organization my company had just bought to determine who was worth keeping. An alumna of my college walked in who had blown me off, pretty rudely, thirty years before when I asked for help networking. I recognized her instantly. She didn't know who I was. Not going to say what happened, but it didn't help her. True story.*

Summary

- It is highly unlikely you will get a job by just sitting behind a computer and sending out résumés.
- It is highly unlikely your friends will find a job for you.
- Sending out résumés AND asking friends to help increases your odds significantly: you can't job search eight hours a day every day.
- There are other activities you can add to your job search time to increase your odds of success. You can make a period of unemployment look impressive to potential employers and valuable to yourself.
- Follow at least the first three structured tracks as I've laid them out.
- Set reasonable goals for yourself in each track and be accountable each week to these goals.

- Keep your pipeline of activities in these tracks full, even if you are sure an offer is imminent. You never know.

- Keep your expectations in check. It almost always takes longer than you think for emails to be answered, interviews to be scheduled, decisions to be made, and offers to come through. While sometimes the length of time you are waiting to hear news of how your candidacy is progressing is, in fact, a reflection of your chances of proceeding; more often than not, the time lag has nothing to do with you. And it is rare for you get a straight answer as to what is going on.

- Sometimes things don't work out, even when an offer seems imminent. When the verbal wink-wink of an offer evaporates, there is absolutely nothing wrong with you or your candidacy. Really. Companies are not sororities or fraternities. They run on budgets that shift, approvals that can be withdrawn, and priorities that change quickly—all of which happens without any consideration of the quality of the candidate who has been interviewed for the role. See above for reasons to keep your expectations in check and your pipeline full until you have a WRITTEN offer.

PART III
Gain Insight

Chapter 9.
Understand the Hiring Process

The hiring process itself can be one of the most confusing and frustrating aspects of the entire job search. Expectations and timelines are rarely made clear unless the interview is with a very well-defined recruiting machine that channels many new graduates into its organization every year like clockwork and has every aspect of the process extremely well-organized and articulated. Very few organizations operate like this. Most recruiting processes are quite haphazard. Overall, wherever you are applying, try to remember that the people on the other end of your résumé are generally overwhelmed with work and are doing the best they can.

Most roles, even entry-level roles, become available because employees leave without warning (this is known as headcount replacement). When this happens, work ramps up dramatically for the remaining team members who need to cover the work of their "minus one." Other roles that become available are the result of a need for expanded headcount, which happens when a team or department is so overwhelmed with work that it needs to hire someone for a new role to help them out. Either way, the people at the company who most need the time to fill out paperwork, coordinate with HR, and leave time in their schedules for interviews are the very people who have the least time available. This means the people who need to review your résumé, schedule time to meet with you, get together afterwards and discuss your potential to be a good addition to the team, then find the time to let you know what they think—have extremely little time to do so. Additionally, like all of us, they also have personal lives where things like vacations, family emergencies, doctor's appointments, etc., can render them even less time. So that extra week they are taking to get back to you? It's very unlikely the result of that one thing you said about deli meat you fear made them think you're an idiot.

There can be an additional multitude of reasons why the almost certainly lovely people who work in HR and in the operating roles at the company where you are interviewing can seem like they are ignoring you. They are not.

In this chapter I'll explain what happens after a company receives your application and what you can expect most often as a first contact. We'll talk about the process of in-person interviews. (Be patient, we will discuss the strategy and tactics for how to approach interviews in depth in Chapter 11, Ace the Interview.) We'll also review the online testing programs, which are increasingly becoming part of the overall application process, and why they should not be a part that gives you cause for concern or the need to study. Offers, everyone's favorite part of the process, but sometimes a tricky part, are on deck after that. For each stage of the process, a section on what to expect and a few tips are included. Finally, you will find a useful list of overall process FAQs—questions I hear frequently but don't necessarily fit into any of the larger categories I've addressed.

So, let's talk about the application process itself. Applying is usually straightforward. You either upload your résumé directly, or upload your résumé to be parsed into the company's applicant tracking system (which may take a little massaging). Hopefully, you are also allowed to submit a cover letter or answer a few qualitative questions about why you are interested in the role and believe you can add value. If possible, also submit your original cover letter and résumé as an attachment in a single file.

Occasionally, an organization will give you clues about ways to get your application noticed by suggesting ways to answer direct questions. Be yourself in these answers, be upbeat, and take clues from what you find in publicly available information. Try to match your tone to what you find, for example, in the employee bios you see on the site or on LinkedIn. (I discuss the types of questions you will find and how to answer them in greater depth in Chapter 6, Develop a High-Impact Cover Letter.)

JerseyCoachAmy: *You may get the odd "Describe yourself in two sentences," or "What would you be if you were a holiday?" question. (Okay, I made up that second one, but it's interesting, right? I'm Fourth of July, FYI.). At any rate, don't try to "game" a question like this. The company wants to see who you are as a person. It's a gift that allows you to put a bit of yourself into the application. In other words, don't write that you just looooove working late or making coding breakthroughs. Say something about the real you. Try to stand out. (Don't use my Fourth of July line. Dibs.) Don't TRY to be funny or intellectual or cool. Be yourself.*

What Happens After You Apply?

Once you send your application into an organization, the application can take a couple of routes before it sees an actual pair of eyes. It may go through an ocular reader to be scanned for key words that match the job description (See Chapter 6, Develop a High-Impact Cover Letter). The first ocular screen may even be done by the original ocular screening equipment: eyes. After the initial screen(s), applications are segmented into categories that are some version of "worth following up" and "probably not a fit."

The "worth following up" applications get forwarded to an actual person in most cases, although sometimes it's a still more sophisticated AI screen. Candidates will drop out along the way. Eventually, if the match is close enough to the needs of the role, a human will reach out to schedule something with you. In many cases this next screening will be a phone call or an online conversation. All candidates that do not make it to the preliminary screen have been relegated to the "probably not a fit" category at that point.

The "probably not a fit" applications will sometimes go to a person whose role is to say thanks, but no thanks; or the applications may be fed into an automated process that generates a similar email and then files your application where there is a slight chance it will come up in an internal search for someone with your skill set.[1] Sometimes there is no process at all. There's a plan to develop one someday when someone has time. In this last scenario, which unfortunately feels like *most* to many applicants, you will never hear anything.

However, another reason why you may never hear back is that you don't necessarily fit into a "thanks, but no thanks" category; you got into that electronic file on someone's desk with a "Plan B" label or similar, indicating that you are not getting called in for the first round of interviews, but you may get called in if none of the first round of candidates who have been selected to proceed works out—which is, effectively, a dead end. But what would they tell you if they reached out? There is nothing concrete to say.

Sometimes, something completely random could happen like the screener notices you went to Penn State and that you may have known his colleague who sits on another floor, on whom he has a crush. He sends off your résumé to his colleague hoping it will result in some renewed correspondence but, alas, he is blown off. Now your résumé is out of the pile of résumés that need a response. Seriously, stuff like this can be the reason why you don't receive any notice that your résumé

---

[1] Personally, I've never heard of this happening. While entirely possible, it would require a greater level of staff, IT, and process continuity than most organizations possess. That said, keep knocking. Eventually, someone may let you in. Enthusiasm matters.

was seen and reviewed. Honestly, the reason why you did not hear back could be one of ten thousand reasons. And in many cases, the reason is not because you would not have made a very good candidate if you had more than six (sometimes, fully automated) seconds to sell yourself into the role.

So, take heart! Someone or some AI program has taken a few minutes to review the work you did. If, never having met you, that entity decides not to pursue you as a candidate based on what you have managed to distill of yourself onto one page it is not a referendum on your life or your chances of getting a job sometime soon. Really, I know I've said this in almost every chapter, but I can't say it enough.

Try not to let your opinion of the company be tarnished if an application disappears into the ether. If the CEO could reach out and thank you for your interest, they would—with sincerity. It is important for said CEO to be able to attract candidates. Companies, like everyone and everything in this world, are imperfect.

If you do get the nod to move forward, you could get a call as early as the same day you apply, and you could get one in three months. Reasons for the delay could be as varied as a holdup on getting a budget approved for the position (jobs can often be posted, but the funding is not ultimately approved or is later denied), to a member of the interview team going out on family leave unexpectedly, to another candidate going through the process to the offer stage and then turning the offer down. You never know.

JerseyCoachAmy: *If there is so much randomness in the process, how do you protect yourself? You finish one application, congratulate yourself, and then start another one. Like I said, it's a numbers game.*

First Contact (Most Likely a Short Screen)

Not all companies start with a screen. Some go straight to in-person interviews or Zooms. Whatever they do, it is the preference of the company and the standard policy they have set up; it doesn't have anything to do with you as an individual.

Your initial contact will most likely be with someone from HR or a recruiter hired to help with the administration of the hiring. The person will likely be more junior and have a checklist of things they need to review to pass your candidacy on to the next stage. Some of those things may be technical in nature (e.g., Is this person able to describe a time when they used SQL?) and some are likely to be akin to what we have already discussed: Do you understand the job? Can you do the job? Do you want the job? If you prepare answers to and examples for those three questions, you can't go wrong. You'll find more on that strategy in Chapter 11, Ace the Interview.

There are times when an initial screen will be with a potential peer or a hiring manager. These may be more conversational in nature, and you'll want to have more questions prepared about the nature of the role, the kinds of projects you would be working on, and what it takes to succeed in the role. Similarly, you'll want to integrate some of the best examples of yourself shining on a similar project or team role into the conversation.

For any initial screening, review Chapter 11, Ace the Interview, and prepare some basic answers about yourself. Take the initial screen seriously: it will be a more narrowly focused version than later interviews where, as a candidate, you will be tested on both your skills and professional behaviors in greater depth.

What to Expect:

- Once you hear from a company and are told there is an initial screen prior to a live interview, the screen will be set up quickly and likely be scheduled for thirty minutes.

- You will be given the name and, in most cases, the title of the person who will be calling you. Check out their position on LinkedIn and prepare accordingly.
- If it's an HR screen, you can probably expect some behavioral questions ("Tell me about a time you_____") and hear a more detailed description of the role.
- If it's conducted by a peer or a manager, plan to ask more and specific questions about the role, so you will both demonstrate strong interest and come away with a better understanding of the job. Know the background in advance of whoever is interviewing you by peeking at their LinkedIn profile. Prepare to talk in a more conversational style than you would in a question-and-answer format.

A Few Tips:

- Going long is a good sign, ending early is not. [2]
- If this is a true screen, there will likely be a set of questions that the interviewer will go through that is asked of all candidates for this position at this stage, with little room for variability. If you are talking more informally to someone in the department, the tone will likely be more conversational and/or informational.
- Prepare as you would for any interview (as outlined in Chapter 11, Ace the Interview) even though the initial screen will not be as in-depth as follow-up interviews.
- The most important question you are likely to be asked at this and any stage will be, "Why do you want this job?" Have an answer rooted in the specifics of the role as relates to your interests and past experiences.
- Check GlassDoor.com to see if there is any knowledge to be gained from past candidates but take what they say with a grain

[2] Unless the interviewer specifically apologizes for having to end early due to a commitment. One sign of a good interview is if the interviewer loses track of time.

of salt, as no one has the exact experience twice. Companies check GlassDoor, too, and like to mix up the questions on you.

- At the end, ask what you can expect for next steps. Note that you are entitled to know next steps/what to expect next at every stage of the hiring process, and *you should always ask*! Why torture yourself wondering?

- You may also ask for feedback on how you did and if there is anything you can do to strengthen your candidacy. Sometimes you will get a good answer, sometimes you will get no answer at all, but it's worth a shot!

- Because there is only one person making the decision at this point, and it's a low-stakes decision whether to pass you on or not, you will likely hear back quickly as to whether or not you will be invited to go forward to the next round.

- Fire off a "Thank you for your time—I remain extremely interested in the role" email immediately. Mention something specific you discussed.

- It's okay to email again or call if you have not heard about next steps in three to four days. If they say "you'll hear in a week," give them a week and a few days.

Subsequent Rounds

These should be scheduled quickly once you are invited, but that is a norm and not a rule. If there is a delay, do not take it personally. A delay means someone important to the process is on vacation, there are a big round of meetings coming up, or a big project is due. Continue, and this is important, to work additional job leads up to and after your interviews. Anything can happen, and you don't have a job until you have a written offer.

What to Expect:

- Subsequent interview rounds will likely be twenty to thirty minutes each, and you will meet with your interviewer one-on-one or in a panel setting.
- If an interview goes short at this point, it is not necessarily a bad thing. The interviewer may have decided right off the bat that you will do.
- Also, do not be surprised if the interviewer appears to have just been handed your résumé on the way in the door—that happens more than you realize. Again, it's the people with the least time who most need to hire someone. This can be a good thing (see Chapter 11) as you can take the lead in the conversation and steer it in the direction you want to go.
- You can expect that the interviewer plans to learn about you by asking questions first, then turning the tables to allow you to ask questions. But don't be fooled! The quality of your questions is a test to see how much you know and how well you might fit in. You need to put time and thought into your questions, even if they are open-ended, because the interviewers are likely to ask you for clarifications. For example:

YOU: "Tell me about what a typical day is like here."

INTERVIEWER: "Do you mean a day with a client meeting, or a day where we are holding internal meetings, or when it's a project-focused day?"

> **JerseyCoachAmy:** *Do your homework. You don't want to get stumped.*

- If you have a panel or group interview, the key thing you want to do is pick up on and become a part of the group dynamic. Try to make eye contact with everyone while you are speaking; be sure to contribute to the conversation but don't dominate. In general, try to enjoy the personalities in the room. This is likely going to be more of a "see how you fit in" discussion than a hard-core questioning by the group, so try to relax (take deep breaths, and try to connect on something personal if you can). The colleagues you are meeting with should be enjoying getting the time to sit together with you in a low-stress situation (for them!) for a few minutes. Personally, I would seriously reconsider whether I wanted to work there if they did not seem happy or no one laughed with a colleague throughout the session. Speak confidently with examples if they ask you in-depth about your skills and how you could support the work of the team.

- Don't be surprised if you go in for a second, third, or even fourth round. Not everyone is available on the same day. You may be asked to first meet the more junior people before you will be passed on to the leaders, or vice versa. Every company has its own style. Follow the advice above for all rounds.

A Few Tips:

- If you have two, three, or even five interviews in a day you can ask for a break— everyone appreciates that you are in a stressful position, so go ahead and ask for a bathroom break or coffee or water if the organizers forget to offer.

- Once you have a schedule of whom you will be meeting and for how long, check out their backgrounds and work through Chapter 11, Ace the Interview, to prepare your talking points, answers, and questions.

- As with the first contact, always ask about next steps. Do not leave the office or end the virtual meeting until you understand the hiring timeline, otherwise the wondering will drive you crazy.

- You should leave understanding who is your one main contact. It might be the HR person who set up your interviews or did your preliminary screen. If you don't know who your main contact is, ask one of the people who are interviewing you, as they will know. Your main contact is the person to ask questions of about the process. Do not be shy. Their job is to tell you what to expect next.

- Try to collect a business card from each person you meet so that you can follow up with them. If you are on an electronic teleconference platform like Zoom, ask people if you may exchange information by text v-card, or follow up with your central point of contact for emails. Use these cards to send thank you emails, fast. Do this by end of day if you can, but make sure you send these thank-you notes by the end of the following day, for sure. Make them short, but in each one, note something specific that you discussed with that person. The conversation you had is more likely to stand out for the interviewer from the three or four other candidate interviews they may do that day. Shorter is better—one paragraph that indicates your gratitude, enthusiasm, and calls out one point of hopefully memorable discussion is all that is needed.

- Don't expect anything back: they will not want to give you any indication of where you stand until everyone has had a chance to discuss your candidacy.

- If you haven't heard anything within the time frame that your main contact outlined, wait a few days (three to four) before you reach out. They will let you know why they need a little more time or give you other news. In either case, you have the right to ask. Don't read anything into whether an answer comes right away or in a few days; at this point, it is just the style of your contact person.

A Note on Time Delays:

If get an offer from another firm (and ONLY if you get a _written_ offer), you can let the company know and see if they can expedite the process for you. Otherwise, you have no say in how quickly or slowly things proceed. You may be experiencing how well- or poorly-organized the company is, especially if they are not contacting you about things in a timely manner at this stage. If so, this is something for you to think about in _your_ evaluation of _them_. However, if the interview stage moves slowly, there can be a lot of factors including time of year (vacations, budget season, corporate presentations), project schedules (technology upgrades, client deliverables), or other time-sapping issues that push interview schedules and new hire sign-offs lower on the priority list.

About Testing

Personality, work style, and other types of online tests are commonplace now, so don't be surprised if you are asked to take one during the hiring process. Testing used to be limited to drug use and typing. That changed when software entrepreneurs saw an opportunity to link the commercialization of artificial intelligence (AI) to the staggeringly consistent research data indicating that traditional hiring processes can cost companies huge amounts of money because they are riddled with bias and can't accurately measure skills or cultural fit.

Technical assessment platforms are now widely used and can assess anything a company feels is important to them, including:

- communication skills,
- personality,
- psychometrics,
- workplace motivations,

- a wide range of office behaviors,
- core values,
- abstract reasoning,
- quantitative and qualitative analytical skills,
- cultural fit,

—to name a few. These are in addition to job-specific skills, such as: coding, Microsoft Office, database query language, or other skills that may be required for a specific role. A company may adopt one or more of these platforms to benefit its overall workforce development in: recruiting efficiency, candidate diversity, employee retention, future skills needs, or candidate experience.

What to Expect:

You'll likely be given the name of the platform, the purpose for the test, and the nature of the testing (e.g., multiple choice, short answer, etc.) in advance. If not, you have the right to ask. You can also find out more online once you know the name of the platform on which you'll be taking the test. If you are going to be taking a skills-based test, you'll want to practice those skills and maybe find a few timed exercises online to get comfortable with the environment.

If the test is to learn more about your personality type or your behaviors, there is nothing you can do to prepare but relax. Tests are usually self-scheduled within a window of time, so be sure to find a time when you know you won't be interrupted and also in a place where you will be comfortable and focused.

A Few Tips:

- Often, these platforms will have a free test available online as part of its sales process, and you can register for it for free. This is good practice and will show you what is being tested (e.g., subject, skill) as well as what your results say about you to your potential employer.

- You really can't cheat these tests, and you really can't game them. Honestly, they do a pretty good job of identifying whether this will be a role and an environment in which you are likely to thrive.

- Be your best self on the test. Don't try to be what you think the company wants you to be or say what you think they want to hear. If it's not the right environment for you, you don't want the job. A sample question could be: I am most comfortable in an environment that is (a) competitive, (b) collaborative, (c) supportive, (d) made up of individual contributors. The correct answer may be "competitive" to fit in at this company, but you thrive in a supportive environment. But who knows? Maybe it is a supportive environment, and they want to keep out anyone who is competitive. It's not worth trying to game it. That may not be what you want to hear, but consider these kinds of screening questions a gift: they will save both you and the company a lot of misery and frustration.

- Ask for the results of your test regardless of whether you go forward in the process. You have the right to see what they learned about you, and it will be worth learning something about yourself and the testing platform.

References

Generally, checking references will be one of the last steps a company will take prior to extending you an offer; you will be asked to provide two to three references from nonfamily members at the final stages of a hiring process if it is headed toward an offer. Remember, however, that until you have a *written* offer, you don't have an offer at all.

What to Expect:

At this point, you'll be asked to fill out a form or send an email with the names and contact information of your references if you have not already done so at the beginning of the process. If you have already submitted your references, complete with contact information, you will likely be given a heads-up that your references are being contacted so that you, in turn, can give them a heads-up.

A Few Tips:

You'll want to make it as easy as possible for your references to give you a shining, detailed account of your best skills and attributes. Provide them with a reminder of the work you did together as well as a brief description of the job to which you are applying so that they can tailor their comments to the kind of skills you used and will be using.

You'll find a detailed overview, as well as a template, about contacting and requesting references in the companion workbook.

About Offers

Offers will be made to you verbally and then followed up in writing. Do NOT exhale entirely, try to negotiate anything, or put a down payment on a home or a car until you have the offer in writing. Trust me on this.

At the time of the offer, all you need to say is "Thank you very much, I'm very excited about the opportunity and I need to discuss the details with my family/spouse/significant other." You are under no obligation to accept the offer at that time. My recommendation is that once you have received, reviewed, and fully understand the package: sleep on it.

Recruiters may ask you to respond immediately, ask if you have other offers or are interviewing elsewhere, and generally pressure you to sign. That is technically illegal. Your offer will likely come with an expiration date, what's known as an "exploding offer," but it will absolutely include enough time for you to fully review the detailed package.

> **JerseyCoachAmy:** *Don't do ANYTHING or tell ANYONE outside your immediate circle until you have a WRITTEN offer. Don't negotiate with your current company until you have a WRITTEN offer. Don't start buying things with your expected new salary until you have a WRITTEN offer. Don't start burning bridges at your current job* until you have a WRITTEN offer. *You have nothing until you have a WRITTEN offer. Seriously. Verbal offers can and do disappear.*

What to Expect:

The offer package will likely come in several files by email and possibly followed up with a hard copy via USPS. You will need to sign, date, and return specific documents by a certain date. If a return date is not indicated, follow up with your main contact person and ask when an acceptable time would be to respond. Review everything carefully, discuss things with others in your life whom you trust, and potentially get advice on negotiating your employment package.

A Few Tips:

When the offer arrives, review it carefully. Beyond the salary number, make sure that you understand:

- The healthcare benefit options, including how much will come out of your check every week to cover the package you want
  - This includes prescription benefits, benefits that allow you to pay for medical-related expenses with pretax dollars that

offer real savings, and other types of similar benefits that someone may need to explain to you but that can be very valuable.

- Tuition assistance—if it's important to you
- How vacation time accrues, and if that time can be rolled over from year to year or expires at the end of each year
- When your first salary review will occur
- Whether you are going to be a permanent employee, or if you are going to be entering on a trial period
  - If you are entering on a trial period, are you clear what the parameters are on which you will be judged at the end? This is critical and an area where a lot of companies fall short. For example: If you will not become a full employee for thirty days, do you know EXACTLY what goals you need to achieve to convert to a full employee at the end of thirty days? Do you need to hit a sales target? Are there specific skills you need to demonstrate? Are there key people that need to sign off on your full employment? If so, do you know what they will be looking for from your performance? You have a right to know this when you start. Your HR contact may be able to get it for you in advance, or you may be able to identify it with your manager and/or internal clients once you begin the job. It may not be the most comfortable conversation, but it is a better conversation to have at the start of a new job than at the end of one.
- Whether you are exempt or nonexempt, which basically means whether you are allowed to earn overtime pay
- Whether or not taxes come out of your paycheck, or whether you need to save for them (Generally, you can assume taxes will come out of your paycheck, but not always and not if you are a contract employee.)
- And any other issues that may not be clear to you

Make a list of all the questions you want to review with your contact person. If you fear that some of these may be "dumb" questions, review everything with someone you trust beforehand. Generally, though, HR people have (1) heard it all and (2) understand that they have entered you into a world of legal jargon that is not intuitive, so no need to feel self-conscious. Chances are very good that they have heard just about every question imaginable at least once before. This is *your* life: own your offer package and how much influence the details are going to have on your life going forward.

Later in this chapter we'll discuss how to negotiate your offer, but for now what you need to know is how to set up a call with your main contact to do that. That person will let you know whether you'll be negotiating through them or directly with your hiring manager. It *is* possible that the negotiation will be with both team members, with some agenda items pertaining more to HR and others more relative to the specifics of the role.

If you need some wiggle room regarding the date your offer expires because you are balancing another offer, go ahead and ask for extra time. But the company will know what you are doing, and no one likes being made to feel second choice. They are not allowed to ask why you want an extension, so you don't have to have an excuse. But be careful to only ask for extra time if there is something important hanging in the balance. Another job offer? A potential promotion in your current role? A proposal coming in to be the next Avenger? Seriously. Important.

On Start Dates:

You will be assigned a start date in the offer letter and will likely have been told in advance what that date will be. There may be wiggle room here if you want a little more time to enjoy life before you start working or have an event coming up. You can ask.

If you have a prepaid vacation on the books or a scheduled medical procedure coming up after you start, now is the time to let your manager know. These things are normal, and your manager will usually not mind scheduling around them with enough advance warning. You may not be *paid* for the time off if you have not earned any yet, but you will not be causing any ill will. On the other hand, if one of these events comes up as a surprise later, you may cause damage to an important relationship. If in doubt, share any commitments now. Honestly, everyone takes time off so it's not that big a deal. And you're a new employee so they want you to be excited about joining them.

Next up: negotiating. While I understand that negotiating may be even scarier than networking, it is an important and expected part of the process. A couple of misconceptions I'll clear up right now:

- Negotiating is *not* inherently confrontational
- Negotiating is about getting what you fairly deserve, not about what anyone else is getting
- If one party is not willing to negotiate, you're done

Hopefully that makes it a bit less intimidating. We're going to go through the process step-by-step. You've got this.

Basics of Negotiating

You should absolutely always negotiate. Fighting smart for yourself is a good indicator of how you will fight for the company, so don't be shy. Negotiations do not always yield results but are always worth trying.

There are many schools, techniques, and tactics for negotiating salaries. A quick internet search will reveal a plethora of resources for free and fee—everything from short articles, to semester-long courses, to degrees. I encourage you to find something that potentially works for you for more sophisticated negotiating in professional situations. But for your first few offers, the most basic steps will never fail.

As always, a little preparedness will go a long way. Before you are ready to begin any kind of negotiation, be sure to:

1. Create a comprehensive list of every issue you want to cover. You don't want to discuss salary and vacation now, then come back in three days and try to get a better title. Frankly, it's annoying to have employees keep asking for more and you are less likely to get what you want every time you come back to the table. Put everything you want up for discussion in one conversation. You may find out that something that is important to a company (such as bestowing upon you your own, rather than shared, office space) may not be that important to you, so you can use that as leverage for gaining more vacation time.

2. Know how important each one of those things is to you. You may want to rank, but not share, everything on your list from highest to lowest priority.

3. Quantify everything on your list if you have not done so already (e.g., What is your ideal salary?).

4. Define three scenarios for outcomes of the negotiations. Remember the three numbers we talked about defining for the job application? (see pages 209 to 210) These three numbers are a version of those, just more refined now that you have an actual baseline:

- Awesome: You get everything that's important to you on your list.
- Good: You're happy; you managed to improve on the original offer.
- Fair: You moved the needle, although not as far as you had hoped.
- Neutral: They were not open to negotiations.

You may be assigned to negotiate with your contact or your manager. They may tell you off the bat the offer is standard and final. If there is wiggle room, send your list in advance (without prioritization or numbers) as the items you would like to discuss. They will likely let you know which things are negotiable and which are not.

For anything that is negotiable: You want to argue for yourself on your merit. You need to propose arguments that you are worth the extra investment because you bring more to the table. Be specific. Give examples of how you have proven yourself to really improve outcomes, to be a valued team member, or to follow a quick learning curve.

> **JerseyCoachAmy:** *You do not want to argue that you heard a friend of a friend in the same role makes more than you were offered, or that you made more at your old job. Those kinds of comments will shut down the process entirely. Negotiate on the grounds that you are worth the money. Period.*

The truth is that the organization likely has a salary band (or range) for the role you are in, and you want to argue that you are going to be so good in that role that you should be at the top of the salary band. If they can't give you the salary, can they trade off with work-from-home days or something else on your list that is important to you? Try to negotiate with other things on your list.

If those tactics fail to get you more money, ask to have your first performance and salary review on an expedited schedule of three or six months instead of six or twelve months. Just remember that you'll have to perform to a higher standard once you set this expectation.

You'll find a negotiating worksheet in the accompanying or downloadable workbook (www.jobcoachamy.com/shop).

It's possible that you may not be able to do better, but you should absolutely try. Women, especially, need to make the effort. A study by the National Bureau of Economic Research indicates that one reason for the gender pay gap may be that when there is no explicit statement that wages are negotiable, men are still more likely to negotiate than women are.[3] According to a Harris Poll conducted for CareerBuilder

---

[3] Andreas Leibrandt and John A. List, "Do Women Avoid Salary Negotiations? Evidence from a Large Scale Natural Field Experiment," National Bureau of Economic Research Working Paper No. 18511, November 2012.

in the spring of 2017, however, new hires miss out equally on potential salary bumps by taking a company's first offer. The study indicates that more than half of workers do not negotiate job offers, but that most employers typically offer lower salaries than they're willing to pay for entry-level roles. More than a quarter of employers surveyed said that their initial offer is $5,000 or more below what they are willing to offer.[4]

Process FAQs

1. How long does the entire hiring process take?

A typical scenario is to get a call or an email response within a few days of applying and then go through a series of interviews in approximately two weeks (longer in the summer or over the holidays). The written offer will then take another two weeks or a month, depending on how much paperwork remains to be done after the interviews, how many sign-offs are required, and generally, how large the company is. Larger companies will typically require more bureaucratic approvals and each one adds a little time.

Based on anecdotal evidence within my own practice, a professional job search will last on average between three and six months for a recent graduate.

2. Is there anything I can do to make the process a little shorter?

Typically, the process will be shorter if

- the searcher has a good network and good networking skills,

---

[4] The national surveys were conducted online by Harris Poll on behalf of CareerBuilder May 24–June 16, 2017 (which included representative samples of 2,369 full-time employers and 3,462 full-time US workers across industries and company sizes in the private sector) and August 16–September 15, 2017 (which included a representative sample of 2,257 full-time employees across industries and company sizes in the private sector).

- and is searching for something that is in direct alignment with his or her experience to date.

The process tends to be longer if the job seeker

- doesn't put in the work every week of applying and networking,
- and has trouble being enthusiastic in interviews because they are interviewing for something they don't really want.

Like anything, you get out of a job search what you put into it. Really doing your homework up front and targeting what you want makes a big difference. Enthusiasm shows. Authenticity counts. If you are applying for sales in high-tech but your heart lies elsewhere, your journey will be harder no matter what is on your résumé. Applying, networking, and spending time on professional development research, as discussed in Chapter 8, can also help shorten the duration of your search.

3. Should I stop applying for jobs once I think I'm getting close to an offer?

There is only one reason to stop applying for jobs: you have a *written and signed offer* for one that you want. Here are some examples of times when you should NOT stop applying for jobs:

- *"I applied for one and I want to be sure I'm available if they call me for an interview."*
  The likelihood of getting one interview from one application is low. The likelihood of getting more than one interview at the same time with no flexibility is, precisely, null.
- *"I had a really good interview and I'm pretty sure it's going to come through."*
  This is an easy trap but a bad one. You never know what is going to happen until it happens. The road to a signed offer can end even AFTER a verbal offer has been presented. There is no verbal

affirmation or "wink, wink, nudge, nudge" in the world strong enough to ensure you an offer. Remember this: whoever happens to tell you "You're in" has a boss with a budget who might say, "I understand you want this hire, but it's not happening."

- *"I never heard back after I applied to a few jobs. I can't take any more rejection for a while."*

There are a couple of reasons for never hearing back, and none of them have anything to do with your value as a candidate or, certainly, you as a person.

- Jobs are often posted for a short time for legal reasons even though the hiring manager already has a candidate in mind or will make an internal promotion. Résumés submitted for these jobs are discarded or "kept on file," but are not usually acknowledged.

- Submitted résumés are batch processed; segmented into "review further," "keep for another role," or even, "show to Brooks, as they went to the same school." Rarely are a group of résumés sorted out as "no" at one single time, which makes it difficult for any one individual to be assigned accountability for notifying candidates that they are no longer being considered. Sadly, even if you call in to find out what happened, there may not be a single individual who knows exactly where your candidacy landed in the process or why.

- You can still make a call and you may get a real answer. It's worth the effort.

4. Why does the hiring process take sooooo long?

The hiring process can just take a long time. HR time goes by at a way-faster pace than Job-Seeker time. And Hiring Manager time sprints at a rate that is even faster. It's not that they are not empathetic to what you are going through, it's just that filling the role is one of fifty-four priorities for HR, and one of 108 priorities for the Hiring Manager. Getting a job is your main goal, but filling the job you want can go on and off the front burner for everyone else. Also, as much as you may be needed on the team, finalizing the details of getting everyone's opinions and getting an offer together may still be outside the boundaries of what MUST be done in a day's work to keep things running.

Hiring someone is an expensive and important decision. Making the wrong one can have significant negative consequences, so the trigger doesn't get pulled without a great deal of thought. Hang in there. And don't stop applying to other places until you have a signed offer.

5. "I'm not sure I want to work for Company A, but I have an interview there next week."

Go to the interview and give it your best shot—you can decide AFTER you have the offer if you want to work there. Candidates reject themselves for positions more frequently than anyone else does. Are you on the fence because the commute looks too complicated? When you go to the interview, you may find that the people who work there are so great that you don't care if you must walk barefoot in the snow uphill both ways to get there. Go for it. You never know.

6. "I really want to work for Company B, but I don't start interviewing until next week. Meanwhile, my final rounds for Company A are this week."

You can't negotiate with Company B for an expedited interview schedule until you have a written offer from Company A. Once you do, you have all sorts of leverage and should let Company B know your timeframe has changed. Tell them when you need to decide and ask if they will move up your interviews. But nothing can happen until AFTER you have a written offer.

7. What if I get this job and I don't want it?

You should still go for it! What a good feeling for YOU to have the decision-making power! If you get the offer and turn it down, don't worry about the company. There will be plenty of people happy to take your place that are also in the interview chute. They would rather have you turn down an offer than show up for three months and decide to quit.

8. If I'm getting a contact who will forward my résumé internally, should I still apply online?

Yes! It shows you have genuine interest in the position and makes it easier all the way around for your contact and for HR.

9. When can I ask about working from home? Benefits? My own career path and opportunities for advancement?

Until you have your written offer, do NOT bring up any of these topics. Once you have your written offer, you can ask whatever you want and negotiate these points. You can likely get an idea of what the answers to some of these questions may be on GlassDoor or similar sites that provide background information on companies. Once you have your offer, make a comprehensive list of all your questions and negotiating points as pointed out earlier in this chapter. Sending things piecemeal weakens your position.

10. What shall I put on the application for my desired salary?

The truth about what you need. You can check to see if there are any guidelines publicly available on GlassDoor or Salary.com. However, before you start the job search, you should have identified these three numbers:

"Woohoo!" Number	With this number, you can put aside the loan payment and still get the apartment you want and the gym membership and the car lease and save a little and take vacations . . . or whatever your top priorities are.
"That Works" Number	This is the salary that will get you out of your parents' basement, but you'll need a raise before you must worry about renewing your passport for that awesome vacation or signing for a new car lease. You can make it work.
"I Can Get by for the Experience" Number	This money is not what you had hoped for, but it is manageable. You're still going to be on a tight budget, but the investment in your future career this job offers is worthwhile.

The delta between those numbers should not be more than $10,000 at entry levels. Write in a number that's closer to your goal number. It might be higher than what they have to offer, but if it is higher by only $5,000 or so they will likely still consider you.

If none of your three numbers align with the salary offered by the job to which you are applying or considering, why bother? You would just be wasting both your own time and the company's time.

11. What shall I put on the application for available start date?

The date you are available to start. If you are working, put in the date two weeks from the date of application. Even if you are not working, that is a good strategy and a good date to pick. You can also write in "ASAP" if the answer field is free form. The point is, you want to show enthusiasm for starting, however you choose to do that. If you are working and have a vacation in a week and could then give two weeks' notice—use three weeks from the date of application. Don't try to incorporate how long the interview process could take or overthink it.

Summary

- Not all companies are good at communicating with candidates who fall out of their hiring process. Many companies can also be slow or even disorganized when trying to shepherd the ultimately successful candidates through their process. Try to be patient and keep applying to other jobs until you have a written offer that you want.
- While all companies vary, the overall process will follow some form of initial screening, followed by live interview rounds and then an offer. The process may proceed in fits and starts. Be patient and expect the process to take longer than you think it will take.
- If you fall out of the process at any time, you may or may not receive an email saying the company has decided to proceed with other candidates that more closely meet the needs of the position. If you receive one, you are allowed to call and ask why you have been removed from consideration. I recommend you do so and hope for constructive feedback.
- If several weeks have gone past the date when the company said you would hear something, I recommend you get in touch with your contact to try to get information.
- Negotiate once you have reviewed all aspects of your offer. Be clear before you start about: (1) what you want to improve (based on the comprehensive list you have made), and (2) how you will negotiate for these improvements based on, and only on, the value that you will bring to the role.

- There is no standard timeline for anything, so try not to get discouraged. Take a short break if you need one. You may go three months without a single bite, then have a great offer in three days. You never know. Keep applying. Keep developing your network. Keep learning about your chosen field or industry. It *will* happen.

Now that you understand the process, lets dig into how you can really make yourself stand out as you go through it.

Chapter 10.
Stand Out from the Competition

If you want to really stand out from the competition, it will help a lot to understand how the company you are interviewing with makes money, and how the role you are interviewing for contributes to how the company makes money (grows) and how it saves money (grows more profitable). In general, all jobs relate to doing one of those two things.[1]

As I *may* have indicated at previous points in this book, the two most important questions to answer in any interview are: (1) "Why do you want to work for this company?" and (2) "Why do you want this job?" Once you've gotten the nod to start the hiring process with any company, your best shot of coming out a winner on the other side is to develop a good understanding up front of why the company and the job exist. So, before we tackle interviewing in general, I'm going to show you how to do just that.

We did this on a preliminary basis in Chapter 6 by focusing on the key words a company uses to describe an ideal candidate. In Chapter 11, Ace the Interview, we'll review the job description in the context of *your* candidacy. In this chapter we use the job description and some basic company information to tell us why the company is in business, and why, specifically, this role exists within the business. The easiest way to

---

[1] There may be times when the job you are interviewing for will relate more directly to *planning* for how the company can make more money or save more money.

understand this is to identify the organization's customer, market, and competition. You'll see examples of how to do this both for profit and mission-driven, or non-profit, organizations.

Next, we'll review exactly why you can't judge a role by its title alone. Through real life examples, we'll look at how the same role at different companies can be very different, emphasizing how important this exercise is even when you think you've got a handle on what you would be doing in a particular role. To finish up, we'll walk through an example of how to decipher a not-so-easy-to-understand business and role. You'll find an additional example of a not-so-easy to understand business and role in the accompanying workbook on my site.

Why You Need to Analyze a Company

Imagine that in an alternate universe, companies sign up for slots to come and pitch their available jobs to you. You get to select a short list of companies with whom you want to meet from hundreds of potential employers. You also get to choose the lucky companies that get a second round with you, and so on. In this scenario, there are way more jobs than candidates, and companies are doing all they can to catch YOUR attention. Essentially, the companies are sending you *their* résumés and cover letters. You are picking from dozens of jobs to find the one that will be best suited to you and will make you happy. What would *you* be looking for from recruiters in a sales pitch?

Here's my guess:

You would want the company to indicate why they want YOU, over other candidates.

You would want to know why you should pick THEM over other companies.

You would discard anything that seemed generic, didn't stand out, or seemed like the company wasn't genuinely interested.

Imagine the difference between:

"Louisa, we know that we want someone for this role who recently earned a college degree and good GPA, preferably an athlete, to join our team, and you fit the bill."

and

"Louisa, we know that you worked hard at academics and hockey in college as proven by your 3.4 GPA and four years playing on the varsity team. We know you can do a great job as a corporate finance trainee with any of our competitors with your outstanding math skills and accounting courses. We all really like your midwestern sensibilities, knowing that you come from Minneapolis. We'd love to have you join our team."

Which one do you think Louisa would pick? My guess is the one that knew more about her and took the time to find out. Perhaps she also appreciated the fact that they knew she was from Minneapolis. Companies feel the same way. They want you to make them feel special.

Beyond impressing the company, you want to understand what you would be doing in a new job, so you're not surprised by things when you show up the first day. Don't laugh. This can easily happen. Let's say you are signing up to interview for a training program at a major consumer products company like Proctor & Gamble. The role is to support the sales of their dishwashing products for one of their southeast regions. What does this mean exactly? Supporting sales could mean:

- Working with publicly available information to identify retail outlets like grocery stores that don't yet sell Proctor & Gamble dishwashing products and giving this information to the sales-people in the field, so they know what stores to target
- Working with sales reports to identify low-performing sales of dishwashing products (i.e., which products sell poorly) within

the region and developing incentive programs to increase sales at those specific outlets

- Fielding calls from retailers who are unhappy because the inventory they ordered arrived late or damaged, then working to resolve the issues on behalf of salespeople

But it turns out that *this* role is about driving a company car to retailers (mainly grocery stores) all day, almost every day with a trunk full of product and promotional displays so that you can

- check how the products are placed on shelves,
- talk to the loading dock managers to make sure new shipments are being placed on shelves in a timely manner,
- review upcoming marketing promotions with district marketers and sales managers (such as coupons that will be running in store flyers),
- and provide store managers with related in-store displays as needed.

This job may sound like a lot more fun than sitting behind a desk all day or it may sound awful to you. Wouldn't you at least want to have this level of understanding about what you would be doing on a daily basis in advance?

Job Descriptions: A Jumping-Off Point

A job description is a great jumping-off point. But job descriptions can sometimes unintentionally obscure what a company and a job are about by using words that make perfect sense *only if you are already doing the job at the company*. Digging a little deeper is always a good idea, and we'll cover exactly how to do that now.

Job Descriptions are almost always structured in five parts:

- Description of the organization
- Description of the role
- Description of the responsibilities
- Description of candidate requirements
- Overview of benefits, mention of ADA compliant facilities, physical requirements, etc.

We're going to walk through the first four sections individually. The last section will be of interest to you, but the information it contains is not something that will help you in an interview or be something you would even bring up in an interview until you have a written offer.

How to Analyze a Company

The goal of this section is to learn how to break down the description of an organization into your own words. Often, you will already have a grasp of the company going in if you are familiar with its products and services (e.g., Starbucks, the Gap, Apple). Additionally, some companies are very straightforward about their purpose. It's a safe bet that a digital marketing agency works with other organizations to market their products or services digitally, and that a food truck company sells food out of trucks. Others, though, aren't so easy to figure out, especially if they serve a less visible market or customer. Still others just load up their overview with a lot of marketing language that doesn't explain exactly what they do.

> **JerseyCoachAmy:** *While it's not always easy to figure out, you really need to know what a company does. Seriously. Don't gloss over this part.*

Here's a job description for an entry-level customer-care role from a company called Altisource[2] in Georgia:

ARE YOU READY TO WORK AT ALTISOURCE?
- *Do you have excellent business acumen with a strong process mindset?*
- *Are you ready to be a key player working side-by-side and being mentored by senior Sales Leaders?*
- *Are you looking to enter a program to accelerate you into a day-to-day management role at one of the leading companies in our industry?*

If so, nice to meet you; we are Altisource! We are seeking an energetic, highly skilled self-starter who thrives in dynamic and fast-paced environments. This NEW POSITION offers an exciting opportunity to learn from the top of the organization. The optimal person for this role brings the combination of business acumen, process orientation, and analytic mindset to drive transformation.

We believe that hands-on experience and mentorship supplemented with classroom learning from our Executive Leaders is the most effective way to develop our leaders of the future.

Sounds great! But it does not tell you exactly what the company does or what the new role will ask of you, does it.

If you were interested in interviewing at Altisource and happened to be lucky enough to have a contact there, you could ask for help to learn a little more about the company. If not, you would need to learn how to learn about the company on your own using publicly available resources. One quick methodology is to learn to identify three key characteristics—the organization's market, customer, and competition—in order to answer the question "Why do you want to work at this company specifically?"

---

[2] This company is real; I have modified the job description expectations and requirements from a real posting.

Customer, Market, and Competition

As mentioned a couple of times already, every organization has a customer, a market, and competition. These three touchstones are easy to figure out for companies like Verizon who serve us (consumers) with access to Wi-Fi and digital calling (market) by providing products we use every day, and purchase over their competitors (T-Mobile, Sprint) for reasons that are easy understand (quality, price, brand loyalty). Figuring out the three touchstones gets harder if the product is made to solve a business need you never knew existed or is in a market you've never thought about.

Back to our example: a quick visit to Altisource's website reveals that the company has three lines of business:

1. Providing technology and services to companies that service real estate loans or mortgages
2. Providing technology and services to loan originators
3. Hosting an online community, called owners.com, that connects real estate buyers and sellers

Now, using this basic information, delve deeper and answer the following questions in the three categories below to help yourself prepare even further for the interview:

Category	Key Questions	Altisource Research
Market	How does this company make money? What valuae does it offer?	The market for this company is real estate mortgages. Altisource sells their customers—businesses that create and service real estate loans—software for the systems and processes that make it easier for them to ask for, track, and deposit mortgage payments. Its systems also simplify the loan application process.
Customer	Who exactly is the customer? Does the company get paid directly by the end user? Or is there a business in the middle?	There are three main customers who likely pay the company: • Companies that service mortgages: the business between the person who took out the mortgages and the business that lends them the money. • Loan originators: the companies who are working with consumers or commercial real estate developers to complete the loan process and then get the loan

Category	Key Questions	Altisource Research
		• into the hands of a bank or other financial institution that wants the debt. Sometimes, but rarely, the loan originator is the same person who winds up owning the mortgage (loan) because they want the stream of income that comes from the mortgage (loan) payments. • Buyers and sellers of real estate who want to connect with each other online, generally cutting out the real estate agent's fee. The buyers or sellers may pay a fee to the website, but the customer is likely the mortgage originators who have access to the portal to identify buyers who are good potential mortgage customers.

Category	Key Questions	Altisource Research
Competition	Who else offers this product or service, and how does this company compete against them?	A quick visit to Owler. com or Comparably. com reveals that their main competitors are Assurant, Guaranteed Rate, Lending Home, and Fidelity National Financial, who also provide systems to companies that service debt, although not exclusively mortgage debt. In this case, a further breakdown of Altisource's products reveals more details of competition. Capterra. com comes up in an internet search and identifies Al-tisource's three main products: REALTrans, REALSynergy, and Foreclosure Bankruptcy Soft-ware. This site also identifies competitors on a product level, which allows you to begin to compare, or at least formulate questions about, the differentia-tors in the products.

Other ideas for identifying what a company and/or its products actually do:

- The "About Us" section of the company's website
- The information found at the bottom of one of their press releases, also usually available on their website
- Wikipedia.org
- Bloomberg.com, Reuters.com
- An internet search for the name of the company + industry
- An internet search for the name of the company + product names

Definitely read any recent general news stories that come up. It's not a good idea to mention general news stories in an interview if they are not flattering, but you want to be aware of them.

Now, in your own words, try to answer these questions based on what you learn about a company you're researching:

- In your own words, how does the company make money?
- How does the company differentiate itself from competitors (your best guess based on what you've learned)?
- What makes the company interesting to you?

Use this exercise to help you build your answer to the question "Why are you interested in working for this organization?" Here are a few possible answers for our Altisource example:

"I'm specifically interested in working at Altisource because I like the idea of leveraging technology to improve what historically has been a burdensome and labor-intensive task for all involved."

"I know that Altisource makes the process of getting and keeping a mortgage simpler, and I would like to be a part of that."

"I really like the idea that you are selling to financial services companies; I'm very interested in working with the financial services industry, as there is so much software being built and integrated into that sector of the economy right now."

A few of the many ways that companies can compete in their market:

- On prices—
  - Walmart and Costco compete against other budget retailers on price.
- By focusing on "verticals"—
  - For example, providing high quality linens and towels only to the hotel industry or manufacturing seat cushions specifically for the airline industry.
- By customer "segment" or differentiated group of customers—
  - For example, Microsoft, as the name implies, started out building software for micro or personal computers; Oracle Corporation focuses on building software for large companies or enterprises: enterprise software.
- By way of their brand—
  - Chanel (a luxury brand) and L.L.Bean (an outdoor sports brand) can charge premiums for their products based on the characteristics associated with their brand. A Chanel purse is more expensive than a purse that looks the same but has no logo, because the non-branded purse offers no prestige. L.L.Bean boots cost more than a pair of unbranded rubber hunting boots because the brand offers its own cachet of quality craftsmanship and durability. Very different brands, same ability to extract premium prices for their products.

About Mission-Driven Organizations

You can do this same analysis with any organization. Even nonprofits and other mission-driven organizations operate with markets, customers, and competition. For example, UNICEF (the United Nations International Children's Emergency Relief Fund) is in the market of providing supplies, shelter, medical care, and any other type of support that children who lose their homes because of war, famine, or natural disasters may require. Its customers are those children (and their families) who seek safety, health care, and refuge. Their customers may also be the governments or nongovernment organizations that serve those children. Even UNICEF has competition, however.

To be in the business of delivering emergency relief, UNICEF needs to raise funds to purchase and deliver that relief. Ergo, they are in competition for charitable donations with other relief organizations, as well as all other charitable organizations asking for support (e.g., Save the Children, the Red Cross, The American Cancer Fund, museums, hospitals, pet shelters, environmental groups, political campaigns).

So just like every other organization, UNICEF needs to market the benefits and impact it delivers to be successful. (Note: In providing relief and comfort to displaced children around the world, UNICEF is truly a cooperative organization and not a competitive one. At the same time, UNICEF is as savvy as any Fortune 500 business in stretching its donated dollars in order to provide as much help as possible to those who need relief the most.)

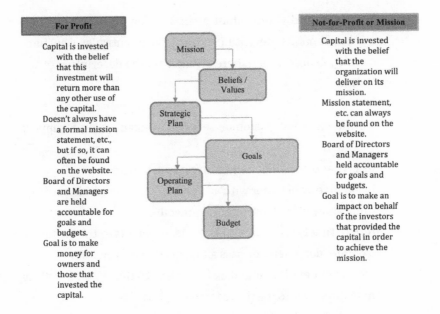

Some companies can be more difficult to analyze than others, often because their product is used for a commercial application that lies far behind what a consumer sees. Companies understand this, and they understand that it may not be easy to grasp exactly what it is they provide and to whom by reading a job description. However, grounding your analysis in understanding of customer, market, and competition can always get you close enough to be able to ask a question that shows you tried. You will earn points for trying.

How to Analyze a Role

Responsibilities

Figuring out what your job would be is far simpler than figuring out what a company does. This is because the second and third parts of a job description tend to be clearer and way more straightforward. The description of the role, often called the Responsibilities or Minimum Expectations section, will usually offer specifics and list the requirements and responsibilities in a straightforward manner, often using bullet points. Revisiting our Altisource entry-level customer-service role job description, here is part two, the description of the responsibilities:

- Provide excellent customer service by establishing a rapport with clients
- Receive and prioritize requests from customers
- Respond to a customer with all pertinent details within the time frame allowed by departmental procedures
- Initiate timely telephone calls, texts, or emails to the customer to obtain, document, or pass along needed information
- Document details of client calls while with the client, inputting them directly into the database via keyboard for future review
- Ensure that work is accurate and complete, processed in a timely manner with proper spelling and grammar
- Perform any additional functions needed to meet the goals of the department

Analyze these responsibilities by translating what you find into three things: (1) what you would be doing daily and/or what your tasks would be in the role, (2) how that will help the company, and (3) what examples you have that can showcase the skills described should you be called in for an interview.

Note that while "receive and prioritize requests from customers" is a straightforward description, you would have no idea what those requests would be about unless you understood what the company does. In this case, you know that Altisource's customers are financial institutions or mortgage originators using their software, and they will likely be calling with technical issues or questions that require user training. It would be very different if Altisource provided a physical good, and customers were calling to find out where their orders were or to return orders.

For our Altisource software job, below is an example of how to break the descriptions of responsibilities into language that describes what you would do in the job and what skills and/or experience you would need to leverage. The last column is left blank for you to jot notes as if you had landed an interview for this job.

Job Description Responsibilities	Best Guess at Daily Activities	Skills, Experience Needed	Example from my background (If interviewed)
Provide excellent customer service by establishing a rapport with clients.	Talking with, getting emails from disgruntled clients?	Good at building relationships, gets along well with people.	
Receive and prioritize requests from customers.	Getting *ad hoc* questions from customers about their product, bugs, how to work certain features, etc. Knowing to work on the highest value orders and customers first, start the ones that will take the longest quickly.	Good judgment, ability to distinguish what is urgent from what is important.	

Job Description Responsibilities	Best Guess at Daily Activities	Skills, Experience Needed	Example from my background (If interviewed)
Respond to a customer with all pertinent details within the time frame allowed by departmental procedures.	Follow training on department rules for timing but also be accurate: be able to work fast without mistakes.	Works quickly and efficiently with a high degree of accuracy.	
Initiate timely calls, Zooms, texts, or emails to the customer to obtain, document, or pass along needed information.	Make sure things don't fall between the cracks or don't sit around because I'm not sure what to do. Keep pushing things forward by whatever means possible.	Takes initiative to complete things in a timely manner.	
Document details of client calls live, inputting them directly into the database via keyboard for future review.	Multi-task: do accurate data entry while talking to the customer at the same time.	Comfortable multi-tasking, detail oriented.	

Job Description Responsibilities	Best Guess at Daily Activities	Skills, Experience Needed	Example from my background (If interviewed)
Ensure that work is accurate and complete, processed in a timely manner with proper spelling and grammar.	Can use English well and can write without making mistakes— double check work.	Works quickly and efficiently with a high degree of accuracy, has excellent written communication skills.	
Perform any additional functions needed to meet the goals of the department.	When I finish my work, ask other people if they need help with theirs.	Good attitude, willing to support team members as necessary.	

Requirements

The third section, Education and Experience, lists the requirements the company believes a successful candidate will need in the role. The third section is also likely to have a bulleted list. This one might be somewhat more generic. Below is part three of the Altisource role—the description of skills and experience the candidate will need:

- BA/BS from an accredited school
- Excellent written and verbal communication skills
- Is a team player
- Wants to be on the forefront of helping to develop new ways to use technology

Note that both the "About the Role" and "Skills/Experience Needed" sections describe elements of "who you are" and "what you'll do." The details of what they provide will vary widely, but what you need to know will always be in one or both of these sections.[3] Prepare for there to be some overlap between sections but treat them equally.

Following are some examples of how you might want to prepare for the interview using this information. The last column is left blank for you to jot notes as if you had landed an interview for this job.

Job Requirements	Best Guess at Daily Activities	Skills, Experience Needed	Example from my background (if interviewed)
BA/BS from an accredited school	NA	NA	
Excellent written and verbal communication skills.	Lots of talking and writing to both customers and colleagues.	Prior jobs and coursework involving lots of talking and writing.	
Is a team player.	Needs to work closely in teams, both as a leader and as a follower.	Project work, teamwork— athletics could be a good example, or group projects.	

[3] We won't go over the fifth section, overview of benefits, as those items generally cannot help you analyze a company and job or prep for an interview.

Job Requirements	Best Guess at Daily Activities	Skills, Experience Needed	Example from my background (if interviewed)
Wants to be on the forefront of helping develop new ways to use technology.	Going to be around new technology development a lot and will need to be interested; the culture is probably very techy.	Proven interest in technology: reading, attending conferences, ability to talk about prior advances in tech.	

With this analysis, you should be able to create a potential answer to the question "Why would you want this role?" specifically. Potential answers could include:

"I enjoy working with people on teams to resolve issues. It's the kind of experience I enjoyed most about school and that I would like to recreate in the workplace."

"I'm good at tackling an issue and running down the solution, pulling in data and information from a number of sources. Working with your customers to resolve issues with the software you sell and help make improvements to the software based on customer feedback would be an area where I know my skills will be helpful."

"I've worked in loan servicing and loan origination in internships, so I understand basically what is involved and I know that technology can improve the overall process greatly. I really want to help improve the industry by making the process of getting a loan and making payments on it easier for the end consumer."

Once you understand what the mortgage servicing software business is about, you will probably have a good handle on how to analyze another company in the same business. However, the same does not hold true if you are applying for a similar role in a different business. The objectives and tasks of roles with the same title can vary widely at different companies, even at different companies within the same industry!

> **JerseyCoachAmy:** *This is an important point too. "Marketing" can mean running quantitative analysis on how effective the same digital banner ad was on getting clicks on two different websites with different target audiences, and it can also mean wearing a sandwich board while standing on the corner and passing out flyers. Pay attention.*

Example: Same Role, Different Companies

Let's imagine you live in Dallas, Texas, and you are interviewing for two marketing roles: one at Interstate Batteries and one at Stryker Medical devices. You have a degree in marketing and you understand one company makes car batteries and the other makes hospital equipment. You understand what both products are—so you should be good, right? You learned that both companies are looking for their successful candidate to have

- understanding of B2B or B2C marketing,
- recently earned a degree in marketing,
- an interest in staying in Dallas long-term,
- skills in using marketing to grow revenue or have experience with top-line growth.

Essentially, the Minimum Requirements section reads the same for both jobs.

Your plan is to tell both interviewers that you want to work in marketing that supports top-line growth (sales), stay in Dallas, and use your marketing degree for a company that helps people (a battery maker, a hospital bed manufacturer).

But let's take a look at how much better your answer could be if you understood the customer, market, and competition of each company.

Interstate Batteries' website[4] says they are America's #1 Replacement Battery *"proudly empowering businesses and households with top quality batteries, industry expertise, and superior customer service. Our business is powered by a distributor network of 300 wholesale warehouses and backed by more than 200,000 dealers around the world as well as 200 all-battery center franchise stores."* Their product list indicates a wide variety of customer segments and battery types—from commercial automotive to household appliance.

So Interstate Batteries has two main customers:

- Households (B2C) that are interested in finding and replacing specialty batteries on any type of home-use product, including tools, appliances, and medical devices.
- Businesses (B2B) that people come to for battery replacement service including car dealerships and other car and truck repair shops.

A quick internet search on the keywords "after-market" and "battery" reveals that the company's competition is other commercial battery makers to those segments. Competitor names include Superior Battery and Crown Battery.

Their B2C marketing is likely aimed at amateur electricians, and their B2B marketing is likely aimed at professional manufacturing

[4] See www.interstatebatteries.com

groups. Maybe they purchase ads in magazines like *Popular Mechanics*, or sponsor community events where they can raise their profile with consumers to help drive sales at retail outlets. Maybe they will sponsor a booth at a vehicular engineering conference and extoll the virtues of Interstate over the competition to raise their profiles with manufacturers and car dealers. Or perhaps an inside or field sales force handles customer accounts sales directly with these businesses.

Now let's consider medical device firm Stryker,[5] who (officially) sells patient handling equipment such as gurneys and hospital beds. The customer would be the hospital administrator who has decision-making power for purchases. A quick Google search would reveal some of the company's competitors include Invacare Corporation and Prism Medical. Take a look at all three sites. In this market, the key is to provide safety and functionality. Make some educated guesses about what makes Stryker stand out from the competition.

Interstate Batteries markets to individuals and car dealerships, which generally have twenty to fifty employees. Stryker markets to hospitals that typically have one hundred to one thousand-plus employees. They are actually very different companies, so the answer to "Why do you want this role at this company?" needs to be very different. Knowing the customer, market, and competition for each can allow you tailor your answer to a killer:

"I'm really interested in the automotive market and like that joining you would allow me to do both B2B and B2C marketing, so I could use both traditional business channels and new consumer social media channels," at Interstate Batteries.

Or at Stryker: "I want to contribute to the field of health care and appreciate that Stryker is all about patient safety. The idea of using marketing and sales tools to build long-term relationships with hospital administrators who are the decision-makers about all equipment used for patient care is one that I know I could add value to. Using marketing

[5] www.stryker.com

tools to develop relationships with decision-makers is something I learned a lot about in school."

You would come up with your own version of that answer, of course, but an answer like that would come much closer to getting you that job than answers that did not indicate you had done your homework about the organization and the role. You'll find an exercise for analyzing a job description on your own, as well as a worksheet to use in your own job search in the accompanying workbook.

Summary

- It is important to be able to understand a company well enough to answer the questions "Why do you specifically want to work *here*?" and "Why do you want to work in this *specific* job?" It's essential to do some basic research anywhere you apply in advance of landing an interview so that you can answer these questions for yourself as well as for a potential employer.
- The job description will have a company overview section that will give you a preview of what the company does, but you will often need to find out a little more information to really understand how the company makes money. There are several good, publicly available resources that can help you identify the organization's customer, market, and competition. From that information you should be able to discern enough about their business model to formulate some informed answers to the question "Why do you want to work here?"
- Even mission-driven, or nonprofit, organizations can be evaluated in this manner, as they also have customers, markets, and competition.
- The job description will have sections on minimum expectations for the tasks you would perform and your responsibilities in the role, as well as the requirements that a successful candidate will need. These sections will be more straightforward in style and

more easily analyzed. For each item listed, discern what you can about what you would be doing daily, how that will help the company make money, and what similar work you have in your background that you can reference in an interview to provide (an) example(s).

Leveraging this research framework will set you well ahead of most of your competitors. A candidate who can demonstrate a grasp of the big picture is a rare find. Knowing this information will also make it a lot easier for you to prepare informed questions and relevant examples in advance of your interview. We'll review interviewing in depth in the next chapter.

Chapter 11.
Ace the Interview

At this point you've done a lot of soul searching, left your comfort zone to talk to a lot of people you don't really know, and invested a lot of time building tools. And that work has paid off—you've landed an interview!

> **JerseyCoachAmy:** *Or you just skipped ahead to this page. Either way, congratulations! You have an interview!*

Let's get you the job!

This will be easier if you have not skipped ahead too much as we'll leverage some of the tools you have already created to develop your interview strategy, including key goals and how to answer (what I consider) the All-Important First Interview Question. First, we'll examine what it feels like to be in the hiring manager's shoes so that you can gain some insight into what they are going to be looking for from you. Next, we'll talk about the tactics to use in an interview that indicate you did your homework and understand the company's operations. Other tactics we'll cover in depth are: how to present your experience, and how you can best prepare to both ask and answer questions. Hint: asking and answering questions are equally important. Lastly, we'll have a word about case studies and where to learn more about them for free, and a few of the best interview tips I know.

Strategy

Interviewing is a skill like any other: it can be learned and mastered. That does not mean mastering the skill of interviewing will always result in you getting the job, but interviewing well will always result in your putting yourself forward in the best light. Don't spend time worrying about what you will be asked; that is unproductive. The best strategy is to be proactive and prepare what you want to say.

Key Goals

In Chapter 10 we talked about how to analyze a job description to prepare answers for the important questions of "Why do you want to work here?" and "Why do you want this job?" Once you're in the interview process, you'll need to take that to the next level by using a strategy that conveys three (three!) concepts.

1. That you understand the job:

- What you will be doing every day
- Why you will be doing it
- How this will contribute to the organization's overall goals

Why is this first point important to the organization?

There's a LOT of time, cost, and risk involved with new hires. Bringing on a new employee who in a short period of time says, "Hey, this job is not what I thought it was going to be at all. I don't like what I'm doing, and I'm leaving," is bad for all involved.

There is a lot of risk involved for you in taking a new role as well. You also want to know what you are getting into. It is tempting to get a job, any job, when you need a paycheck. And positive affirmation. And some kind of success in a process that can wear you down. But taking any kind of job just to have a job is not a good idea for you either. Even if you really need to take a job doing stuff you don't like doing, you want to make a well-informed decision in advance.

2. That you can do the job:

- Relate the skills, experiences, or characteristics you have developed to date that can help you do this job.
- Relate how they apply to the team's goals.

Why is this second point important to the organization?

Being able to indicate that you not only understand what the job is, but that you also have the skills to do the job, is the next level you need to pass through for consideration by a hiring manager. For example, if the job description says you'll be working in teams, you will want to get across that you have experience with group projects or working collaboratively. If there will be quantitative analysis, you'll want to highlight your Excel and math skills.

Don't take this to mean that you need to prove you are already an EXACT match for all the skills that will be required. Your interviewer expects that you will need some training and mentoring to come up to speed on the exact nature of the work that is required. In some cases, if you have never done anything like the work required before, that is actually a bonus: You don't have to unlearn habits and techniques that fit in a previous environment but won't fit at this new one. For example, every company has its own internal rules for creating presentations. If you have never done that before specifically, training you from scratch is easier than breaking you from wanting to "do this the way we did it at my old job."[1]

If your specific skills are not an exact match for what the company is looking for, present them as general abilities. How might you do that? See below.

Relevant Candidate Skills—Some Examples

Company Needs	You have	You Can Talk About your General Skills
SQL (Standard Query Language)	Python, R	The ability to learn new software, either off-the-shelf or proprietary,[2] quickly.
B2B sales experience	Retail experience in sales.	Not afraid to take on challenges that involve direct outreach, talking to people, building relationships.
Experience working with large data sets to identify patterns, trends, and anomalies.	Completed a research project at school using publicly available information to create a conclusion.	Very detailed, analytical, always interested in understanding "why," and able to clean, transfer, and manipulate data.

[1] This would be what's known as the "soccer camp principle." If you go to a fancy summer soccer camp and then come back to your school team and try to explain at preseason practice, "Do it this way, the way I learned it at soccer camp," it is fairly likely that no one will listen to you and very possible that you will still be called "Soccer Camp" at your 10th reunion. Be aware that I may be the only one that calls this the Soccer Camp Principle.
[2] Off-the-shelf software is defined as a package you can purchase, such as Microsoft Office. Proprietary software is one that a company builds internally for its own use, and you can only learn it once you are an employee.

3. That you want the job:

- Have a good answer for "Why do you want this job?"
- Seriously, this is important. Be specific. If you have not done so yet, read Chapter 10.

Why is this important to the organization?

If you seem more eager for the role than the other candidates, you are more likely to work harder to do well in it. The role almost always goes to the person who demonstrates that they want the job the most.

JerseyCoachAmy: *This is no time for subtlety: If you really want a role, let your interviewers know.*

Why should this be important to you?

Here's the way final hiring decisions are often made: A meeting happens where all the interviewers discuss the candidates. The hiring manager asks the team what they think and who would be the best fit for the group. Some comments are made, and if there is not one clear winner, then there is usually a discussion that sounds like this:

"Well, these two people seem to be about the same level of ability and fit, but this one wants the job more." And the offer goes to—the person who wants it more. Why? That person is more likely to work harder in the job. While it's easier to be bubbling with enthusiasm in the thank-you note you write afterward, the timing is not as effective. By the time the note arrives, the decision has been made.

Understanding what the job is and what the company does is critical to having a good answer to the question "Why do you want this job?" Let's say you are interviewing three candidates for an entry-level job in the project management department of a company that makes logistics software. Here are the answers you get as to why they want the job:

KEVIN: "I'm well-organized and good with people, so I know that I can do well."

GRAHAM: "I've talked to people in project management and that seems to be a job I can do well."

BRIAN: "I've always been interested in the process of how software engineers translate business needs into code and then get input from customers to test and improve the code, so I know I will be interested in the software development processes that project management oversees—the job will be interesting. I also really like the idea of working in the logistics market because I've always been fascinated by how goods move across the country by rail and train. I would love to have those huge companies using the software that I helped make."

Is it just me, or is Brian getting the job?

Each of the three categories of interview goals has a tool you can use to verbally demonstrate supporting points:

- To convey that you understand and can do the job, use informed questions
- To convey that you can do the job, use examples from your past work, volunteer or academic experience that link to the type of work you will be doing in the job
- To convey that you want the job, be knowledgeable, enthusiastic, and engaged in your words and body language

Objective	Tool/Methodology	Example Talking Point
Show that you understand the job.	Ask informed questions based on your research of the company, the position, and the job description.	"It seems as though you have clients from many different industries. Do you have industry experts in each area?" "In this role, I am guessing that I would spend 50 percent of my time doing administrative work and 50 percent doing research to support the marketing team. Is that accurate?" "The position description mentions accountability for helping the team I support do research. Will that research be online with publicly available information?"

Objective	Tool/Methodology	Example Talking Point
Show that you can do the job.	Use specific examples of work you have done in the past (either academic or in a job setting) and relate them to the responsibilities of the role.	"I know that my responsibility will be to keep calendars current. I have used both Outlook and iCal in my past internships." "The position description mentions that I will need to juggle multiple priorities, and I have experienced what that is like in a campus role I had where . . . ."
Show that you want the job.	Be enthusiastic. If you really want this job, you need to let them know. This is not the time for subtlety!	"I am targeting positions like this one because I love working with numbers and the idea that I will be working for a company that makes something people use every day."

In your talking points, be sure to always add an example. Anyone can say "I've always wanted to work in high tech," but it's much more powerful to add "I started getting *Popular Science* and *Wired* magazines when I was in high school, and I still get excited to download them. I especially like to follow the new products I read about in the robotics space and like to see them show up in products that later become commercially available." Add examples to your statements before the interviewer asks and know that it's likely these questions will be asked.

Why is this important to the organization?

You will be far more credible in meeting any of your three key goals if you have an example.

Key Goal	Statement Without Example	Statement With Example
Show That You Understand the Job	"The job description said this is for a finance role, and I'm great with numbers."	"I know that this department runs payroll for a lot of independent contractors. I am comfortable doing this kind of data entry."
Show That You Can Do the Job	"In all my courses I've worked with spreadsheets, so I have experience."	"I had a summer job at a building site that required me to input all project costs, and I enjoyed that work."
Show That You Want the Job	"I would love to work here."	"I know I want to work in a company's finance area long-term, and this is exactly the kind of job I have been seeking—where I can apply my skills but also learn."

See the difference?

JerseyCoachAmy: *If you can make your interviewer believe that you can come in and hit the ground running right away based on the skills you already have, bingo! Less work for them. Your name goes to the top of their list.*

Why is this important to you?

Your examples are unique to you and provide a great opportunity to make an impression on your interviewer. Your goal is to indicate that you have done the same *type* of work that you would be doing, that you enjoyed it, and that you are eager to learn more about doing the work in the context of their business.

A few other notes:

- It's okay to speak proactively about the points you want to make—you don't have to wait to be asked. Try one of these phrases to introduce a topic:
  - "One other thing I wanted to mention...."
  - "Something else I would like you to know about me...."
  - "One other experience I wanted to share that I believe will help my candidacy...."
  - "Can I tell you about some work I did that was similar to the tasks I would do in this role?" The answer will always be, yes.

JerseyCoachAmy: *This whole "prove you want the job" thing is equally, if not more, beneficial to you. If you can't think of ways to prove that you want this job, you probably don't want it. Save everyone the trouble and move on, or maybe even start over. DO NOT continue to apply for roles you don't really want. It is a death spiral to apply for jobs you don't really want and/or for which you are overqualified. You are unlikely to get these jobs because, in fact, hiring managers can tell your heart is not in it and you will likely not work out or not stay long. Sometimes a client will come to me saying "I couldn't even get this volunteer role or that part-time minimum wage role!" My answer is always "Of course you didn't, because you didn't really want it." Focus on what you want, not on just getting a job. It matters. And your interviewer can tell.*

The All-Important First Interview Question

Of all the questions you will answer in any interview, the most important one will be the first one. The majority of interviewers make up their mind about you pretty quickly. So add to your strategy: prepare a strong and enthusiastic response to, or even to preempt, the All-Important First Interview Question.

The good news is that it's easier to prepare for this question than you might think. Why? Because the first question in an interview is always going to be some variation of:

- "Tell me about yourself."
- "Walk me through your résumé."

Or the more pointed (and my personal favorite)—

- "Why do you want this job?"

Because first questions are generally open-ended, you can set the course for the interview by sharing up-front what you most want the interviewer to know. And because first questions are generally the same in nature, you can prepare for them in advance. This helps both lower your stress level and improve your chances of making a good impression in the first few minutes of an interview, when it really counts.

Start by making a strong statement about why you are interviewing for the job. Stating your reason for interviewing for the role will grab the interviewer's attention right out of the gate. Be positive. Throwing shade is a red flag.

Some examples of solid reasons for interviewing include:

- "Before I tell you anything else, let me tell you that I'm very interested in this job because you have an excellent reputation for integrating cutting-edge technology into your products."

- "I'm drawn to your mission because it is important to me personally, and I know that the customer-relationship development skills I have will allow me to add value in the role."
- "My goal has been to find a role where I can use my quantitative skills in a team setting, and I know that in this job I can find that while I contribute to your new product launch."
- "I have been targeting your firm for a sales role because I've done my research, and I honestly believe you have the best product in this space because...."

Next, address why you know you will do well in the role. Bringing up the strongest and most relevant aspect of your résumé will draw the interviewer's attention there.

- "My academic record shows I am a quick learner and a skilled engineer. I know that I can add value in your environment because of my capabilities and my strong interest in your work."
- "I have a track record of doing a great job managing accounts receivable and accounts payable. Whenever there is something I don't know, I make a commitment to learn the new entry type on my own, then confirm with a colleague that I am using it correctly."
- "Sales is my passion and I've been selling all my life—from on-campus events to internships—and I know I can add value to your firm and clients."

Lastly, close with the idea that you are enthusiastic about the opportunity to interview quickly, and then turn over the baton. Having addressed that you understand the role, why you will do well in it, and how much you want it, you have specifically addressed what the original question might have been. If you feel you need to go through your résumé, touch lightly on experiences working backwards from the present. The interviewer will stop you when they want to know more about a specific area.

As you continue to talk about yourself by citing examples and background data, keep things quick and professional. Small talk is fine if the interviewer encourages that. But DO feel comfortable being quiet.

> **JerseyCoachAmy:** *A little dead air is better than continuing to talk while your interviewer is starting to lose focus.*

DON'T ask anything specific about yourself, such as how quickly you can get promoted or what kind of training you would need. It's not about you until you have a signed offer.

As a bonus, preparing these statements in advance will help quell a lot of interview stress. You know how things will start, and you know you will start on a confident note. Interviews can sometimes be stressful for the interviewers as well. They are going into a one-on-one conversation with a stranger who is probably very nervous. Getting to the point up front can help reduce their stress levels in those first few minutes as well. Who knows? This may be the edge you need to become the lead candidate.

One word of caution about this approach relative to the type of interviewer in front of you. A junior interviewer or HR staffer will have more time to review your résumé, prepare formal questions, or work from a set of guidelines that require specific areas and questions to be covered. The more senior the interviewer, the more likely they will be handed your résumé for the first time on the way in the door.

For the junior interviewer with an agenda, allow them to go through their prepared list of questions. For the more senior interviewer who has not had time to prepare, taking control of the meeting will probably be a very welcome change of pace. The more you tee up a free-flowing conversation for a senior interviewer or hiring manager, the better things are likely to go.

Whether you are opening your interview by answering questions or setting the tone with an opening statement, be wary of chronology. Everyone's natural tendency in this situation is to start at the beginning. For example:

- "I started becoming interested in dentistry when I was just seven," or
- "I grew up in Topeka and came to New York for college."

The problem with this approach is that you are saving your current situation, what the interviewer really wants to know about, until the end, when their attention level has dropped. These answers can give an interviewer the opportunity to tune you out while reviewing your résumé. Or worse, tune you out entirely.

Sure, the interviewer may be interested in where you went to high school or how you became interested in taking STEM classes, but they are not nearly *as* interested in that as they are in knowing, for example, why you are interviewing now. All of which means that your precious minutes of early interview decision-making time are being wasted. Always start at the most recent or current experience and work backwards.

In the Hiring Manager's Shoes

What does an interviewer want from you? Let's think about the hiring manager's point of view. They've been short a colleague for a period of time, meaning they and the team have likely taken on added work to make up for the staff shortfall. This interviewer has to take time away from what is already a crowded schedule to make time for interviews. It's a catch-22 (look it up) for the interviewer, but it's a good thing for you. They want you to be "The One" so they can stop interviewing and get back to work. As mentioned previously, the interviewer wants you to succeed as much as you do.

First and foremost, hiring managers want someone who can make a significant contribution to their goals, make their lives easier, and add value to their team.

If you made it to the interview stage, then you look good on paper, but you also need to display the right attitude and skills live—either in person or virtually. The attitude you need to integrate into your interview is humble, hungry, and smart.[3] The three basic skills that all hiring managers are seeking, whether they are explicitly called out in the job description, are: attention to detail, good organization skills, and the ability to juggle multiple priorities at the same time. As you prepare for your interview, think about integrating these three characteristics into the examples, or "stories," you present from your background.

Show That You're Humble

Why? When you are a newbie on a well-functioning team, you can't be afraid to ask for help or admit to a mistake. You need to demonstrate a certain amount of humility.

How? If you're asked about a weakness or a time that something went wrong, tell the truth. Use a real example.

Why does this matter? Your interviewer doesn't want you to be perfect: they want to know you can admit and learn from your mistakes. Also, don't feel you need to brag about how fantastic you are at everything; that behavior shows an interviewer you are feeling insecure. Even if you know everything (hey, maybe you do know everything in your world), you can't know everything about how your new employer does things. You must be teach-able, or you will be a problem.

[3] This concept adapted from: Patrick Lencioni, *The Ideal Team Player* (San Francisco: Jossey-Bass, 2016).

Show That You're Hungry

Why? An employee who does what they are told can easily earn "meets expectations" on a performance review. What the hiring manager wants is someone who can "exceed expectations," and this means they want someone who is willing to work hard and take initiative.

How? Use examples from your life and career to show that you are eager to learn, work hard, and go the extra mile.

Why is this important? Employees, managers, and leaders who are "hungry" take initiative, pivot when necessary to meet their goals, and generally do whatever it takes to get the job done. Those who are not hungry get stuck or give up. Have an example prepared for a time when you needed to persevere.

Show That You're Smart

Why? This is not just about where you went to school or even how good your GPA was—although, of the two, GPA is more important. This is about demonstrating how quickly you learn and can think on your feet.

How? Try to think of examples to use in your interviews that prove you have demonstrated a fast learning-curve in your life and exhibited good judgment.

Why is this important? Being able to think on your feet, knowing when to ask for help and when NOT to ask for help, understanding things quickly, and thinking two steps ahead are things that a résumé cannot tell an interviewer. However, you can provide examples of your past experiences than can. That could make the difference in setting you apart.

Show That You Pay Attention to Detail

Why? If you make little mistakes that no one catches, your manager looks bad. Your manager does not want to worry about spending time catching and correcting your little mistakes. Ergo, they want an employee they can rely on to NOT make little mistakes. Nor big ones, obviously, but those are easier to catch.

How? Any example will do. Were you the only one who realized you had to hire both a campus police and town police presence to hold a concert when you were in charge of the Big Spring Concert at school in your junior year—and saved what would have otherwise been a disaster? Consider preparing the example. Or were you the only person on the team at your summer job to realize that you needed a permit to hold a sidewalk sale? That is definitely worth integrating into your description of the experience. Why? Because someday you may be the intern or newbie that points out to the team that they are considering a major product launch to moms during a school vacation week, which would definitely have a negative impact on results because it would mean that they would not be spending much time on social media or email.

Why is this important? Everyone has had the experience of having a report go out the door with a mistake, or a presentation get in front of an audience with a critical typo. Prove that you are one more person on the team who can help by citing a time when your attention to detail saved the day in the past—either for yourself, your friends, or your work colleagues.

Show That You Have Good Organizational Skills

Why? If you're not organized, you are not going to be able to support your manager and your team as well as if you are organized. At some point they are going to ask you to find something they've given you or some work you have done, and if you are not well-organized it's going to take longer to find it.

How? In an interview, try to mention a time when you were able to quickly get your hands on a crucial number, file, or data analysis in a previous project. Mention a school, camp, or internship process you reorganized to be more efficient.

Why is this important? The faster the pace is at an organization and the more customer-focused the organization is, the more critical good organizational skills are to success. And all good organizations aspire to be as fast-paced and customer-focused as possible.

Show That You Can Juggle Multiple Priorities

Why? All jobs require you to make a multitude of decisions each day, week, month, and year as to how to spend your time. What tasks are most important? What projects will have the greatest impact, and for whom? Everyone in an organization has multiple demands on their time, and everyone must prioritize how to keep multiple customers happy: internal customers (colleagues, bosses, partner departments) and external (clients, third-party partners, influencers).

How? What may give you an edge in an interview is to work in one of your examples where you have been in this situation before and did not flee from the challenge or have a breakdown. For example: "As an intern for a small consulting firm, I did a lot of PowerPoint. Sometimes the numbers changed at the last minute or the partners would wordsmith immediately before a presentation. It was important for me to stay calm when making changes and note what pages had to be reprinted and changed within the decks. Sometimes I had three or four people shouting changes at me. I needed to stay very focused."

Why is this important? At some point in every job three angry people are going to show up at your workspace demanding something from you within the next ten minutes. It doesn't matter whether your workspace is a cubicle or a corner office, this will happen. You need to figure out how to handle the demands without melting down.

Tactics

Company Analysis Revisited

Hopefully, you've already analyzed the company's job description using the tools we reviewed in Chapter 10. To help you feel as confident and prepared as possible, go back to the company's website to do some homework. The site will tell you what they do and a little about their major projects or products, their clients (maybe), and any advances they have made recently. It will also likely tell you the things on which they are focused as an organization. If they care about an accomplishment or goal, they will put it on their site. And you should know about it.

How much time should you spend? Spend just a few minutes when you are writing your cover letter. Then a little more at each step leading up to your first live interview, when up to an hour may be worthwhile depending on how much content is available.

If the opportunity comes up fast and you need to do a "quick and dirty," try a few of these research tactics:

- Read the company's latest press announcements and/or skim their white papers.
- Read a little about the backgrounds of the executive team and board members.
- Be able to name three to five of their clients or projects or products (depending on the type of company).
  - Follow them on LinkedIn and skim what they have been posting.
  - Read any recent tweets, Facebook posts, and/or blogs on their site.
  - Ask friends or anyone you might know who work there for advice such as—
  - Examples of interview questions (*Note: Websites like GlassDoor can be helpful for finding this information as well.*)

- Any "war stories" about interviews
- What do they think they did right in their interviews to get the job? What have they seen others do wrong?
- When you have the names of the people who will interview you, go to their LinkedIn profiles to get an idea of their skills and backgrounds. LinkedIn will give you deeper insight on how your roles would fit together, and what the interviewer's main interests in you may be.

Why is this important? The best way to prove that you want this job is to show that you have done your research on the job. It's hard to sound genuine with a company about wanting a job with them when you don't know anything about their business, and it is hard to get a job when you don't sound genuine about wanting the job.

Presenting Your Experience

Most people start in the middle when they present their detailed experiences. For example:

"I have really advanced Excel skills from an advanced biology project I did."

Okay, that's interesting. But what would be really interesting is if you explained the project fully, for example:

"In my senior year of college, I developed a model to quantify my research project on the impact of deforestation in Brazil. My goal was to identify what the impact would be of a 1 percent increase in the temperature of Brazil's rivers on the number of insect- and plant-species survival rate. It required a significant amount of data from many different publicly available data sources and a lot of data cleaning, regression analyses, pivot tables, and other advanced Excel skills. As a result, I am comfortable working with large data sets and advanced functions."

The following is a worksheet for presenting your experience in the best light, complete with an example for a sales-enablement project. You'll find a blank worksheet for your use in the accompanying or downloadable worksheet (www.jobcoachamy.com/shop).

Presenting Your Experience Worksheet– Project Example

To speak cogently and confidently about what you have to offer, you'll want to thoroughly prepare a short list of points to get across about your skills and experience. Use this worksheet to help you cull the key factors in your experience that indicate you understand both (1) the big picture and, (2) the value of your own contributions.

Project Example: For an internship with a national "Save the Oceans" nonprofit, you were asked to take the names and addresses of everyone who had donated in the last ten years and put them into a new software to make them searchable by zip code and area code.

	To think about:	**Your Notes:**
Project Goal	*Who funded this project and why?*	The Development Team was doing national fundraisers only, but they wanted to do more specific fundraising campaigns to different areas of the country. However, the database had name and address all in one field so it was not searchable by address.

	To think about:	**Your Notes:**
Project Scope	*Use numbers, geographic parameters, an order of magnitude— anything definitive to describe the size*	There were over 300K names in this database, which was a simple spreadsheet. The company had purchased a fundraising database and all of the data needed to be transferred into it.
Your Role	*Be as specific as possible*	My role was to learn the new software and identify the best technique to transfer the data as quickly and effectively as possible.
Key Issues	*What problems did you encounter in practice? Were you able to make revisions to the plan?*	If all of the data had been entered in the same format, it would have been fairly easy, however, before the data could be imported and parsed, I needed to make a lot of adjustments. For example, I needed to identify whether we would port over "Main Street" or "Main St." I needed a little more time than originally thought to clean up the data, but it made the transfer easier in the end.

	To think about:	Your Notes:
What You Enjoyed About It	*Embed your skills here: loved working with disparate stakeholders, enjoyed the data analysis, loved working with the team to identify key variables.*	It was great to learn what they needed from the software, then create best practices for data entry. I watched how fundraising worked with the ocean scientists, the Executive Team and the Board. It was fun to learn how the different parts of the organization used the data I was working with.
Key Insights	*What was the basic finding? Anything that tells a story and/or may be surprising*	It surprised me how much more powerful the organization could be with more flexible data. For example, a red tide hit the West Coast of Florida while I was there, and the organization could segment its database to let all the donors who live there know that this was one of the things we are working on—and unexpected donations came in! They would not have been able to do that before.

Additional thoughts:

- Does your story hang together, and will the story flow naturally? Change the order of the pieces to make the most sense.
- Are you comfortable going through these points in your own words? Practice.
- Would you find it interesting?

Preparing Answers

Interview questions can be behavioral, job specific/technical, or career-based in nature. For behavioral questions, you want to give examples that indicate you are someone who works hard, plays by the rules, and always keeps the overall goal or end game in sight. Technical questions relate to the job at hand and the knowledge or training you are bringing with you to the role, so you'll want to talk about how your specific experience and skills apply to what you will be doing in the role. Career questions are of a more personal nature, and generally focus on getting to know a little more about you as a professional and individual. Generally:

Type of Question	Objective
Behavioral	To find out what you would be like as a colleague
Technical	To find out how much value you would add as a colleague
Career	To find out a little more about you as a professional and as an individual

Behavioral

Following is a list of behavioral examples and recommendations for answering these questions.

Overall, the best advice is to be honest.

JerseyCoachAmy: *An inauthentic answer is easy to spot. Don't use something cool you heard someone say in an interview or that your brother said you should say. The follow-up will be tough.*

- Tell me about a time that you made a mistake and how you overcame it
  - This is about showing that you can learn and are still learning. We discussed this earlier in the chapter under the concept that managers want employees who are humble (see page 251). In preparing you answer, consider that mistakes are okay; everybody makes them. However, surprises are bad: you don't want to sit on a mistake until it is too late to correct it.
- Tell me something you really liked about your (most recent) job or a campus experience. Tell me something you did not like about it. **Note:** You should be able to answer this about any aspect of your résumé (i.e., all old jobs and schools as well).
  - This can be about a task, or about an element of the culture. It's okay to give away something about yourself in this answer. If there is something about the task or the culture that you did not like in the past that is going to show up in this job, do you really want it?
- Can you give me an example of how you contribute to teams? What role did you play in the team dynamics?
  - It's okay to either be a leader or a good soldier who went along with the norms set by others as long as you can give a good answer as to how you contributed. The answer must be specific about the work you did and how that work impacted the outcome. The only bad answer is something that sounds like you are a non-contributor who takes credit for a team's success and distances yourself from a team's failure.
- What is your greatest strength?
  - As long as your answer is based on something work-oriented, there is no wrong answer.
- What is your greatest weakness?
  - Don't even bother with the answers "working too hard" or "caring too much." Just admit that you know you have

something to work on and be specific about how you are working to put a manual override in place.

- Tell me about a time you did not get along with someone and what you did about it.

JerseyCoachAmy: *No venting. Keep it clean. Don't use any physical altercations, or any story that winds up with you taking the hat off a disgruntled policeman and then just tearing off down the street to show your friends (no reason why that is so specific). You never get frustrated. You never had a bad experience. You just learn and move on.*

- Don't skip the part about why you did not get along with someone in a business context. If, for example, someone did not contribute, how specifically and what did you do about it? Both the "what problems did it cause" and the "how did you fix it" aspects of your example are important.
- Tell me about a time when you were really stressed about a deadline or a pressured situation and how you dealt with it.
  - Again, don't forget about how you got into the pressured situation. And don't blame others. Just explain that you understand how events transpired to land you there. It's a fact of business life and a sign of maturity that you understand things go wrong sometimes, but you deal with it.
- Tell me about a project you worked on and what role you played.
  - See the Presenting Your Experience worksheet on page 257. This question is a really good opportunity to talk about something important in your background and a story that you'll want to prepare. Most people start in the middle or just talk about the end, but in doing so, they miss the chance to prove they understand how the challenge arose, what the barriers

were, and how the solution is having an impact. When you prepare a succinct but complete story, it can make your example a lot more powerful and memorable.

- How would you feel about giving your manager or your customer bad news?
  - The answer is that bad news is never easy to deliver or receive, but it's always best to be straightforward and let someone know as early as possible. Recommending an alternative scenario is a good way to make the presentation if possible. For example, "I would probably be as straightforward and detailed as possible about why the news is bad. Understanding of the situation, not nice words, tends to make the news more bearable. If possible, I would also want to suggest an alternative, or recommendation." If you can, prepare an example of a time where you did this. "One summer I was working on a loading dock, and a particularly important shipment was delayed. I let my manager know that the shipment had been placed on the wrong truck and reported where the mistake had happened, what was being done to correct it, and when the shipment would actually be received."
- Tell me about a time you had to make a hard decision and how you handled it.
  - This answer should always be in the context of what was best for the organization overall first, then your division or team, and finally, the players involved.

Job-Specific and Technical Questions

Job-specific questions are a chance to show that you did your homework about what is required in the role. Mention specific clients, products, or projects you have learned about in your research.

> **JerseyCoachAmy:** *If the question is "Can you program R?" don't answer "Sure!" and then have a staring contest. You want to answer "Sure! I used R program a couple of times in college to run statistics on data sets I had collected in my upper-level psychology classes. It was not hard to learn."*

- "Here is an example of a project we are working on: What do you think is the key problem to be solved? How would you solve it?"
  - Try to relate to tools or methodology you have used in similar situations. Feel free to ask more questions until something clicks.
- How do you see yourself fitting in here?
  - Mention your understanding of the organizational structure, its goals, and how you would interact with your colleagues. Be as specific as possible, mentioning how your skills would apply. It would be fine to ask if your perception is correct or for more information.
- How do you see yourself adding value?
  - Talk about your skills and what you understand to be the company's goals. Be specific. Ask if your understanding is correct. It's okay if you are off a little; how could you know exactly unless you were working there already?
- What do you think will be challenging for you in this role?
  - Be honest, but also state your plan for overcoming the challenge. You will have a learning curve about the organization, so mention that you plan to study what you can—from company goals to products to administrative processes. Will you also need to learn the industry? Get to know your colleagues well to succeed? Let the interviewer know you've given the issue some thought.

- What do you think might come easily to you in this role?
  - Go back to your skills. Give examples.

Career Questions

For career questions, be honest. Want to make a lot of money? Want to be a star in whatever field you choose? 'Fess up. Be sure you indicate you are willing to work hard for what you want, and don't fall into the trap of asking about your potential career at that company if you were to get an offer.

> **JerseyCoachAmy:** *Until you have a signed offer, your conversations need to be all about how you can provide value for them, and not the other way around. Do NOT ask about whether you'll get your own office, if there are free snacks, or if taking a two-hour lunch is frowned upon. (You won't, there may be, and it is.)*

Think about how you might answer these questions:

- Where do you see yourself in five years?
- What is it about this industry that makes you think you will succeed in it?
- What is it about the job or industry that makes you think it will be interesting?
- Tell me what you know about this industry.
- Tell me what you know about this role.
- Tell me why you think you would be successful in this role.
- How do you see yourself adding value here?
- Why should I hire you specifically to help support our goals?

Next, you'll want to think about how you might answer the following potential (standard) questions:

- Why are you looking for something new?
- Tell me what you have and have not liked about your previous jobs?
- What do you want to do in your next role?
- What do you not want to do in your next role?
- What do you do for fun?
- What do you know about this role/this function/what we do?
- Why are you interested in what we do?
- What kind of managerial environment do you do best in?

Preparing Questions

The questions you ask during an interview are key for indicating that you "get it." As a reminder, every organization has a market, a customer, and competitors. You should be able to identify all three at a high level at this stage. If you have not yet done the basic research to understand this about the organization (see Chapter 10 on analyzing job descriptions as well as Chapter 7 on networking), go back and do that now.

In preparing questions, you need to make an effort to understand the big picture: every organization has a market to grow, a customer to woo, and competitors to beat. If you try and really can't figure it out, it's okay to ask during an interview. Some organizations are complex and really do not make it easy to identify what they do in all their various business units. The key is to ask an informed question that indicates you tried.

- "My understanding is that you design and manufacture food packaging to sell to smaller food companies that do not have their own in-house food packaging teams. Is this correct?"

- "How do you compete for business against other food packaging design companies? It looks like there are many other small and some large ones in this city alone."
- "It looks like you have mostly organic food companies as clients for your design and packaging products. Is that part of your company's culture? Would you ever take on more traditional, mass-marketed products?

Other good questions are those that allow the interviewer to envision you as part of the team. Ask questions to get them talking about what happens on a daily basis so that you gain insight about what you would be doing:

- Who will be on my team?
- Who will be my manager?
- How will I be evaluated?
- How will I support my manager's goals? What about *their* manager's goals?
- Who will be my internal clients?
- What will I be doing on a day-to-day basis?
- What makes someone good in the role to which I am applying?
- How can this role best help the interviewer achieve their goals?
- What is an example of a typical task/project?
- What would make this task/project really stand out as excellent work?
- What are the biggest challenges in this role?

Businesses are complex organizations, and all are organized differently based on the detailed specifics of their markets and customers. You don't have to figure out the intricacies of them for the first interview. What really helps, however, is to understand the broad outlines of the job and how it fits into what the organization does. Making some educated guesses is both a good way to figure this out and to impress upon the interviewer that you've been making the effort.

This is where the real payoff comes from the work you did in Chapter 10 analyzing the job description, which included analyzing the company and what you would do in the role. You learned how to answer the key questions, "Why do you want to work here?" and "Why do you want to work in this role?" but you also learned enough to craft informed questions:

- "So, in my role, I will be supporting the marketing staff as they create promotional materials for our products?"
- "My accountability will be to find contact information for sales leads using publicly available sources and then pass them on to business development reps?"
- "I understand I'll be fulfilling the scientists' research requests, how many scientists are in the group, and what specifically are their specializations?"

This is another opportunity to set yourself apart from other candidates by indicating that you understand the role. You can improve upon this opportunity further with a follow-up question that indicates you can do the role.

Informed Question	Answer: "Yes, and...."
"So, in my role I will be supporting the marketing staff as they create promotional materials for our products?"	"I will be good at that: I volunteered at a medical clinic and supported six nurses on staff at any one time. All six always needed three things at once, and I got high marks for staying focused and calm and getting things done."

Informed Question	Answer: "Yes, and...."
"My accountability will be to find contact information for sales leads using publicly available sources and then pass them on to business development reps?"	"I have experience drumming up business. When we sold T-shirts at homecoming, I did not wait at the table we set up but went to every car that was tailgating and took orders then delivered them. We increased sales by over 100 percent."
"I understand I'll be fulfilling the scientists' research requests. How many scientists are in the group, and what specifically are their specializations?"	"I did a lot of this type of research in college for my scientific thesis and became very familiar with a lot of publicly available resources for scientific information and how to manipulate them to find what I want. Also, I used several proprietary but commonly used databases, so I can hit the ground running."

For all three of these examples, you could follow up with:

"I loved doing it! This is one of the reasons why I really want this job!"

Then you would have the hat trick: you'll have achieved all three key objectives by adding that you really want the job.

JerseyCoachAmy: *Duh, the best questions to ask in an interview are the ones you are curious about. Stay engaged with what the interviewer is saying. If some of the discussion resonates with your research, mention it. Ask a follow-on question. Try to engage in a back-*

> *and-forth exchange of ideas. This is the best outcome: the interviewer will start thinking of you like a colleague and stop thinking of your discussion as an interview.*

You'll find a comprehensive Interview Prep Worksheet in the accompanying workbook.

About Case Interviews

If you are interviewing for a consulting firm and possibly some banking roles, you are going to be asked to do a case interview. If you are not planning to apply for one of these highly competitive jobs, please move on, as I do not wish to stress you out unnecessarily. If you are planning to apply for one of these highly competitive jobs, please do more research than just what I am presenting here. This site has a lot of good, free resources: http://www.caseinterview.com. You just need to give your email. The site, however, is intense, so don't let it freak you out. The following is an overview in case you want to start here or just want to know what all the fuss is about.

Case interviews come in a couple of flavors, but the easiest way to think of them is as a question that asks you to structure a response. You are going to address how you would solve a kind of puzzle of sorts and make some "guesstimates" in lieu of actual data. They'll help you along the way as you can talk through it and/or jot down some equations. This is a test of reasoning, analytic framework, and common sense. You need to use reason to turn a question into a math problem. Here's an example:

Q: How many eggs per day are consumed in the city of Boston?

Amy's example answer: "Well, first you have to think about how many people live here. I think it's about a half million. Then you have to think about the visitors who work here or travel here for work or pleasure. Let's call that another 100,000, so we're talking about 600,000 people. Of those, how many will eat eggs for breakfast? I would guess 20 percent, assuming that 20 percent don't eat breakfast and 60 percent eat something other than eggs. So now we are talking about 600,000 x 20 percent, or 120,000. Maybe 1/3 have 1 egg, 1/3 have 2 eggs, and 1/3 have 3 eggs. So, the Math is:

$$(120{,}000 * .33 \times 1) + (120{,}000 * .33 * 2) + (120{,}000 * .33 * 3)$$

Then you need to think about eggs that are eaten in other things like baked goods and eggs eaten for other meals. It's probably fair to say that 75 percent of eggs are eaten as eggs for breakfast in Boston, maybe 5 percent are eaten as egg salad, 10 percent are eaten in batters and crusts as well as in egg dishes at other meals, and 10 percent are in baked goods. So, you can then add to the equation:

$$((120{,}000 * .33 \times 1) + (120{,}000 * .33 * 2) + (120{,}000 * .33 * 3)) / .75$$

Or you could arrive at a number a different way: maybe starting with estimating the number of homes, restaurants, and offices that would serve eggs or items with eggs on a given day. Then add eggs that were sold through grocery stores and eaten that day at home or previously purchased, kept in a refrigerator, and eaten at home that day.

There are lots of ways to structure the argument. The answer doesn't matter as long as you can get to the equation. And the key is to not get flustered but to relax into the issue at hand and try to enjoy it. Case studies are basically riddles. If you don't enjoy them, you will probably not like the jobs behind them.

A more sophisticated case will phrase this as a business issue:

Q: "I'd like to start an organic egg business serving Boston, but I know that I would need to produce and sell at least 100K eggs every day to turn a profit. How do I know if 20K eggs even get eaten in Boston every day?"

And add a follow up question:

Q: "How would I go about starting to sell into the Boston egg market, and how long do you think it would take me to start selling 20K eggs?"

They would be asking for a common sense-type answer such as:

A: "You would want to see how eggs are sold now: By salespeople? On contract? From local growers or big farms? At what price? Are the people and businesses that buy eggs happy with what they are getting? Would they be interested in switching? If on contract, could they switch? Could you put them on contract? Then you would want to add in sales, marketing, and distribution costs based on your answers before you could begin to make a determination."

Note: This is not necessarily a 'correct' answer or a comprehensive one, but hopefully, you get the idea.

A brief study guide on how to structure case interviews can also be found in the accompanying or downloadable workbook (www.jobcoachamy.com/shop).

General Interviewing Tips

- Shake hands and look people in the eye.
- The enemy of enthusiasm is anxiety, which most people feel during the interview process. This is natural, as you are putting yourself out there to be judged. What helps is to remember that the interviewer is ONLY interested in the small part of you—your applicable experience and skills—that you bring to the job.

They are not judging you for the way you treated your mom via text this morning or the terrible breakup you had last week.

- Talk to interviewers like they are a peer, not as though you have been sent to the principal's office.

- Stay relentlessly positive: you've never had a bad experience, just many learning experiences. Not enjoying your last job or your last team or your last boss is a big red flag.

- Be enthusiastic and engaged: lean forward, smile a lot, be the best version of yourself and not the most nervous version.

- Don't try to be something you are not. If you are quiet, that's fine. If you are a big goofball, don't playact at being something else. Authenticity (and lack thereof) is a lot easier to spot than you would think.

- If you want to ask a question but don't think it's appropriate to interrupt, go back to that point in the conversation when there is a break. For example, "A few minutes ago, you said that you like to give people coaching as they go along. Does that mean we would be having weekly meetings to check in on how I'm doing?"

- Your interviewer is evaluating how much you can add to the organization, how much you can contribute to their team's goals, or how much easier you can make their life based on your perceived work ethic. They want to know how trustworthy you may be to complete an assignment well and on time. So, if you know you can accomplish tasks on time—because you did it reliably at school—and work hard when you need to, because there have been plenty of times in your life when you did, relax a little! You are not *actually* on trial.

- You can't get personal in an interview (e.g., "Adolescence was tough for me because I was really into magic and that wasn't 'cool' in my school,") but you can show your personality (e.g., "I spend my free time learning about magic and sometimes I'll do shows for friends. I've just always really enjoyed learning and performing amateur magic."). Show your real personality: authenticity is easy to spot and makes you both likable and memorable. Are you a little goofy? Quiet? Obsessed with a sports team? Let yourself shine through.

- Don't cross your arms over your chest or close yourself off in any way.

- Keep your hands above the table, and don't be afraid to gesture with them if that feels natural.

- During an interview, the biggest pitfall to stumble into is talking too much. When nervous, most people ramble on—and on. Eventually they talk themselves into a corner and wind up exactly where they didn't want to be, such as talking about the job where they got laid off, the manager that didn't like them, and the course they almost didn't pass. Avoid that trap by being concise. If the interviewer wants to know more, they will ask. Silence isn't a bad thing in an interview. Going off topic can be.

- Be appreciative of the opportunity. Thank your interviewers and let them know that the more you learn about the organization and the more you get to know the people—the more certain you are that the role is a good fit for you.

- Send thank-you notes as mentioned previously, but don't wait until after the interview to show your enthusiasm. The interviewers' minds will be made up before they leave the room.

- Spend enough time preparing answers so that you feel comfortable answering some basic questions on the fly in each category. It's really up to you—you'll know when you feel ready. Don't try to script answers- that never works.

- Do what you need to do to feel confident. Try using the voice memo app on your phone to prepare answers and talk about your experiences. Find a friend to do a mock interview with you. If that is not your style, wing it with a friend first, then make a few notes about how you feel it went and how you could do better.

- When in doubt or lost, tell the truth. If you have to lie to get a job you want, it may not be the best fit for you.
- BE YOURSELF. Use this, and any other advice, the way it works for YOU. If you are trying to project something false, it will show.

Your interviewer wants a strong colleague, not a new best friend. I've noticed that, when asked how an interview went, many people will say some variation of "Okay, they seemed to like me," or "I'm not sure if they liked me." Remember, you are not being judged on how likable you are *per se* but on how well you answer questions as a potential employee. It makes a difference to prepare answers that showcase your capabilities as a potential employee.

JerseyCoachAmy: *For God's sake, when you answer questions, use examples. Be specific. Don't expect your interviewer to take a wink and a nod as proof positive that you can get the job done.*

Here are two secrets no one ever tells you when you start out on your career path:

One, your interviewer really WANTS to like you so they don't have to do any more interviews and can get back to work! Having a role open on your team generally means more work for everyone else, including having to review résumés and take time out of the schedule to hire. Be confident! The interviewer wants you to succeed as much as you do.

Two, life is long and industries are small. The hiring manager who interviews you today may be an applicant to lead a team that you are on a year or two from now. This means that it is entirely possible roles may be reversed in the not-too-distant future, and you may be interviewing your interviewer. It happens all the time. That gives interviewers an added incentive to be nice to you and that should give you a boost of confidence when you're looking at the person across the table.

On Getting That Surprise Question

You can't prepare for every question in advance. If a question comes out of left field, your first instinct is probably going to be to tackle it to the ground with so many words that the interviewer will be left dazed and confused. Here are few techniques. Pick one, or a combination, to use instead of that initial response:

- Take a deep breath. Don't just start talking. A pause is fine and will seem much shorter to the interviewer than it will to you.
- Repeat the question to yourself or use some form of "I haven't thought of it that way before."
- Ask a clarifying question:
  - "Are you looking for an example?"
  - "Would you like me to place this in the context of the work you do or the work I have done in school?"
  - "Can you give me an example of the kind of answer you are looking for?"

If your interviewer is good, the surprise question will happen, and you can't really prepare. You need to prove you can do what the question is really asking: think on your feet.

JerseyCoachAmy: *Get a surprise question? Stay calm. Breathe. It will get you more than halfway there. You can say, "Gee, that is one I was not expecting." You cannot say, "Holy Mother of God, are you freaking kidding me?"*

What's an example of a surprise question? Well, by definition—never mind. Here are a few I have heard:

- What would you do with a million dollars?
- What would be on your dream Jeopardy board?
- Running or walking? Why?

Some interviewers just have a "signature" question. Sometimes they make sense, and sometimes they don't. Sometimes they matter, and usually they don't. Know this, but don't worry about it too much.

Summary:

- The three key goals of an interview are to prove that: you understand the job, can do the job, and want the job.
- Remember, your interviewer wants you to get the job as much as you do.
- Do your homework in advance. Be sure you understand the role, how your skills apply to the role, and why you want the role.
- Do your company research in advance. Be sure you understand the organization's market, customer, and competition.
- Prepare to open the interview with a strong statement about why you want the job and how you know you'll add value.
- Prepare the best or strongest experiences from your résumé as stories to showcase during the interview. Include examples in every one of your answers about your skills and experiences.
- Never run out of questions to ask. Stay engaged and ask questions that might arise on the spot. ("You mentioned that you get part of the client's marketing budget to spend. Do they tell you how they want you to spend it, or do you figure it out?")

Interviewing is at the heart of getting a job. You'll likely do it more than once and, hopefully, it will get easier. If you're not a natural, don't worry. This is a skill and skills are learned. Obviously, you can read. Odds are you can also ride a bike, play a sport of some kind, and plan a vacation. You can also in the appendices, revisit Chapter 9 on the hiring process, and Godspeed to you! In the next chapter I'll share my best tips on starting off strong in your new role.

PART IV
Hired

Chapter 12.
This Just Got Real

Hooray! You scored an offer that you want! Celebrate, relax, and pre-pare to start off strong. Spend a little time circling back with every-one who helped you along the way, think about the best way to hit the ground running at your new job, and do a few other things to take best advantage of your "newbie" status. The recommendations I've outlined won't take a lot of work, but they will make a big difference.

We'll review a few things you'll want to take care of before you start (a.k.a. "life administrivia"). I also want to get you thinking like an exec-utive before you've had your first day in a career role: namely, to start taking your responsibility as a salary earner seriously. No one is going to say this to you outright unless your performance becomes an issue. I want you to be ahead of the game and not take anything for granted, so I am going to say it to you outright. Lastly, once you do start, there are multiple things you can take advantage of as a new employee in your "honeymoon period" that you'll want to do before your freshness stamp expires. We'll talk through the "how" and "why" of each one, including how to establish a good reputation early.

I'll also give you the best advice I can on what to expect on your first day in hopes of calming those "night-before jitters" (there's no reason for them) and provide you with a few things I wish I had known when I was starting out and a few tips I couldn't find a way to categorize. I am very old, so I'm allowed to give you some personal advice and tips, but if you want, you can skip that part.

> **JerseyCoachAmy:** *Don't skip that part. That would be stupid. There's key information in there that can make a huge difference in the impression you make in your first days, which will have lasting effects.*

Before You Start

Officially close out your job search by tying up loose ends. This is an easy step to skip, but don't. The effort you put in to get this job is an investment in your network, which is a lifelong asset. Make it a priority to build some goodwill with those who have been involved in your job search. Here's how:

- Call anywhere your résumé is still active and take yourself out of the running. This should be a phone call to your HR contact, which will likely end up as a voicemail. Follow up with an email.
- Send an additional email to anyone you met at the company during the hiring process. Let them know how much you appreciated being considered for the role. They are now part of your network and you are part of theirs—leave the door open for further professional communication. They will appreciate it and wish you luck. Don't feel badly—it's no big whoop to them, and if you are working for one of their competitors, they will be happy to add you to their own network should they jump ship.
- Reach out to your references and let them know you have accepted a role, what you will be doing, and how appreciative you are of their help. This can be as simple as an email or as elaborate as a flower delivery (but do not spend money you do not

have; no one wants that). You are going to want to keep a good relationship with your references. Odds are good you are going to want to reach out to them again at some point.

- Send a note to any contacts to whom you reached out and let them know that you have found something—this includes anyone who gave you time, whether or not it was helpful or led to anything. This can be an email, but a handwritten note is much better. Invest in some good quality plain stationery to keep on hand for business. If you have a birthday coming up, you might want to ask for a professional looking set of notecards with your name printed on it. (I like www.thestationerystudio.com and www.americanstationery.com. Both have reasonably priced options and frequent sales.)

- Update your records while you are reviewing the efforts you made to network during this job search. Be sure you have included everyone, their contact info, organization, and role. You'll want to refer to this both for your own future job searches and to help others that might reach out to you. In the years ahead, send a shout out to any of these people if you see them getting an award, quoted in the press, read an article that makes you think of them, etc. You want to nurture your network. It's always a good idea to reach out when you DON'T need something—that way they are more likely to take your call when you DO need something.

Between getting the offer and your start date, relax and enjoy your time. You want to start fresh with energy and purpose. Complete any outstanding tasks you may have been putting off until you knew you were going to have a salary again. Get your car serviced, your shoes polished, visit that elderly relative—any life maintenance task that will be harder to do once you start working. Identify any changes you may want or need to make based on your new commute too. Do you need to change drycleaners or pharmacies? Get a different commuting pass?

The one work-related detail I recommend taking care of is identifying a preferred method of tracking your goals, achievements, and ideas in your new role. Research software packages if you want to use one or buy a new notebook. Make sure the methodology you choose is one you will *use*, so find what works for you and that you enjoy using.

See Your Salary as a Serious Responsibility

One thing to take to heart when you start a new job is that you are entering into a larger flow of capital within an organization. By drawing a salary, you are taking on a shared obligation to make sure that the money that is invested in the organization (by shareholders, private equity lenders, or any other type of investor/owner) provides a good return on investment.

> **JerseyCoachAmy:** *Stay with me. This may feel like a tangent. It's not. I want you to own this point before you start. It can make you stand out. In a good way.*

If the organization fails to provide an adequate return on the money invested in it through its profits or impact, the organization's investors will go elsewhere.[1] Your manager knows this, as does their manager, and so on up the line. Everyone has a boss, and all the bosses are interested in making sure that the money they are spending is being put to good use. If it is not, and expectations for return on capital are not met, capital goes elsewhere. Doors are shut. Everyone goes home.

Get used to the idea that you are a part of creating a return for the company's investors by adding value through your job. The work you do

[1] The lines between investing for profit and investing for good are not this black and white, as an increasingly large number of investors want their investments to produce qualitative returns such as climate-neutral impact or fair-trade practices. These requirements also place demands on operations.

every day is creating a return on your salary. In other words, (you want to) give more value back to the organization than you take out of the budget with your paycheck. That is the bottom line.

Put yourself in the investor's seat. Let's say you have $100 in your savings account that is earning you approximately nothing in today's low-interest environment. You're telling some of your friends about it in a bar one night and how you'd like to find a way to have that $100 (of capital) make some money for you. Your friend Shane has a business making cheese. But he needs money (capital) to buy ingredients so he can make as much cheese as possible for an upcoming artisanal cheese event. Last year he sold out. This year he knows he can sell as much as he can make. If you give him $100 to buy cheese-making supplies, he'll guarantee you $105 after the show. (By the way, you would be selling him debt, and the deal that you are making is actually to purchase a bond in Shane's business for 5 percent. This fixed-price investment in Shane's business yields you a fixed-rate return. But that's another book.)

Sounds like a pretty solid investment idea. After all, Shane has sold out of his cheese before, so he is likely to sell out again.

Ian is also listening to this conversation. He asks why you are asking for just fixed-price return. Don't you want a cut of the overall profit? Ian says, "I'm making beer to bring to the same show and I'm putting in $100, planning to sell it all for $200. If you also put in $100, we could sell it all and make $400, then split the profits and each double our money. But if there is a ton of competition for home brew and we only sell one-fourth and make $100 in profit, we'll both lose $50." (By the way, this deal would mean effectively buying 50 percent of Ian's business or 50 percent equity, which means there's potential for higher risk but also higher return.)

Suddenly, more people jump into the conversation. Jess would like to use your $100 to start and eventually franchise a new exercise work-out—yet a different investment model. Emily makes herbal teas, and the market is exploding. Matt will split the American Ninja Warrior prize money with you if you can finance his application video. Margaret has an app that can translate toddler cries into the sounds of a soft spring meadow.

Imagine you had enough money to fund all these ideas. You'd be a shareholder, a debtholder, a franchisee, and an investor with endless funding opportunities and endless models. In such a position, would you then be following up with Shane, Ian, Jess, Emily, Matt, and Margaret to see how the ideas were panning out and if you were going to see a return on your money? You're damned right, you would. Would you accept it if one or more was not feeling well and missed a deadline or was waiting for instructions from you to get started? No.

> **JerseyCoachAmy:** *Bars are fun You can meet some real characters. Don't bring a checkbook.*

Simplified Organizational Capital Flow—Figure 1

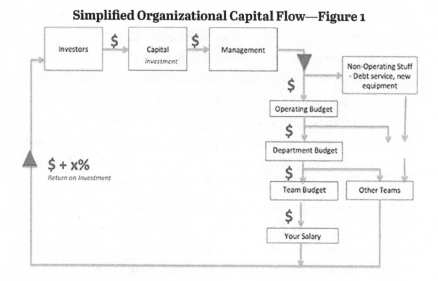

Don't sit in your office and cash a paycheck. Take responsibility for what you earn and how you are contributing in return. There is an endless stream of opportunities into which capital can be invested. Once an organization gets capital, there is a burden on that organization to make good use of the money and provide good returns, or it will go away. And when management pays your salary, they transfer some of that burden to you. Take this responsibility seriously. Do your job well and think about how you are going to outperform your job responsibilities every time you cash your check.

Take Advantage of Your Honeymoon Period

When you start, you will have a honeymoon period that will help you get off to a good start. Take advantage of these opportunities as quickly as possible. Your "newbie" status will wear off over time and you'll feel less comfortable doing some of these things.

- Introduce yourself. When you're a new face, you have an opportunity to meet everyone by saying, "Hi, I'm new!" And you should. You'll make a few contacts in other departments that maybe you would not otherwise meet. These contacts could be helpful as well as just plain fun. People appreciate it when you reach out, and it's nice to know people from other parts of the company, as well as occasionally beneficial. At some point, you are going to be passing these people in the halls or seeing them in the bathroom all the time. And it will be much more awkward to introduce yourself later.

- Create allies. Find someone you may want to ask to be a sounding board for you. In every organization there are quirky personalities in the org. chart and unwritten rules that may not be obvious but could have an impact on your work. You'll want to have a colleague you can ask about any peculiarities you might notice—not on a personal level, but to the extent that it may have an impact on what you, your team, or what your boss may be trying to achieve. For example, is there a colleague that you should never meet with in the afternoon because they are always grumpy? Organizations are made up of people, and people are quirky. You never know what you might turn up.

- Review your role. With your colleagues—some of whom you have probably met in the interview process and some of whom you likely have not—sit down and review the details of what will be expected of you. How will you work together with people in other divisions or departments? What will be important to know? Are some things more important than others on your list of accountabilities? What is the best way to solicit feedback? Ask some of the people you respect around you for fifteen to twenty minutes of their time, or for coffee or lunch if that is supported by the culture in your office. People will respect that you are interested in learning from them in order to do your job better, and you may get some surprising and valuable information.

JerseyCoachAmy: *Just like in fifth grade, the new kid has an aura of mystery. All your clothes are new, and no one knows anything about you. Use this to your advantage before the novelty wears off.*

The most important thing you'll want to do in your first few weeks on the job, however, is to establish strong and clear lines of communication with your manager. Initially, you'll want to have a clear understanding of what your accountabilities are in your new role, how your performance will be judged, and what you will need to do to both meet and exceed expectations. Have your job description with you for this discussion and take notes. Do not be surprised if it makes your manager uncomfortable and allow them to take a few days to get back to you with specifics. But don't let it go—you are allowed to and deserve to understand the answers to these questions.

You will also want to establish a pattern for regular communication. When and how is the best time to check in with your manager? Would it work if you planned to meet for a few minutes before a regularly scheduled team meeting every other Wednesday? Or would it if be better if you emailed them every other Friday afternoon to see what may be on their calendar for the coming week and where you might fit in for a fifteen-minute discussion. You should be prepared to drive the agendas in these meetings so that your manager does not have to prepare anything and make sure they know you'll show up with an agenda.

During the meeting, you'll want to discuss what you are working on and get ideas for how you can improve your work. Ask for coaching and feedback. Discuss any issues you may be encountering and present options for how you are thinking of potentially dealing with them to get specific feedback on tackling problems. Let them know areas that are of particular interest to you and assignments you might enjoy if they come up. Ask for recommendations for additional reading, research, or people to talk to in the organization. Record your discussions in your notebook or software.

> **JerseyCoachAmy:** *No, it's not sucking up if it's your boss. Its investing in getting ahead. Point of clarification: you want to then go ahead and do what they are recommending. That is the difference between sucking up and really being an asset to them.*

Keep a few things in mind, however, at each meeting:

- *Be Formal.* Don't rush someone or ask for spontaneity. You want to be on the calendar. A manager will have a lot on their plate and will need to, at least, mentally prepare for an internal employee discussion.
- *Be Consistent.* Letting go of one meeting without scheduling another is a slippery slope.
- *Be Results-Oriented.* Your priority is contributing to the organization, not selling yourself.
- *Do What You Can.* A five-minute virtual call can make a difference if you can't have a fifteen-minute sit down.
- *Be Prepared.* Have a prioritized agenda and use the time well.
- *Be Committed.* Follow up and follow through.
- *Be Appreciative.* You are asking your manager to make an additional investment in you.

Establish a Good Reputation Early

Here are a few things that you can bet your manager is going to be looking for from you, regardless of what job you have snagged or industry you have entered.

- High-quality work and a good work ethic. So double-check your work, review your work with peers, if possible, do more than what is required, show your work if it is the result of multiple steps or an answer you arrived at after a series of tasks. Your manager and/or team will want to understand how you arrived at your conclusion.
- An ability to pick up processes and tasks quickly so that they only need to be explained once. So ask whatever you want, but only ask once and write down the answer so you have a reference the next time you need to know. Asking all the questions about the copier and the acronyms is another "newbie privilege" that tends to evaporate over time.

- How well you understand the overall goals of your team and your organization. So listen, be aware, and ask.

JerseyCoachAmy: *I know you didn't really need to buy a book to tell you this; its common sense. Jobs are like life- common sense applies.*

Seems like common sense, right? That's all it is. A lot of new grads starting their careers think of new organizations like a black box, but the truth is that success in organizations is just like success in every other part of life. If you work hard, learn quickly, and understand how you fit into the big picture, you WILL succeed. Below are some tactics to get you started in your new role.

Objective	Methodology	Example
Produce high-quality work and demonstrate a good work ethic.	Double-check your work. Review your work with peers, if possible. Do more than what is required. Show your work.	Double-check your work: You want to be known as the go-to person who gets it done right. Run your numbers more than once. Logic-check your statements. If you don't get it right the first time, no one is likely to say anything to you, but they are likely to remember. Review your work with peers, if possible: Ask for input, THANK people for their time, and review any points about which you may not be confident. Explain what you were asked to do and how you did it. Don't expect anyone to read a document for you, but you can boil down the work you are tackling in a couple of sentences and ask someone at the water cooler, in the elevator, or on the stairs. Be sure to ask first, though. If you are intruding on someone's time, you need to be respectful. Do more than what is required: Think about how your manager, or whoever asked for the work, will use the work. Are there other things you can add to the original request that might help? Ask! Be sure that what you are doing will be useful and not wasted effort. Show your work: just like in grade school, the methodology you use to complete your work matters. Make sure it is available in a written format in case you are asked and that you are able to quickly review it verbally as well.

Objective	Methodology	Example
An ability to pick up processes and tasks quickly so that they only have to be explained once.	Ask whatever you want, but only ask once and write down the answer so you can reference it.	<u>Ask whatever you want:</u> When you are a new employee, your status gives you the right to ask just about anything. Take advantage. A mysterious acronym that gets batted around? Ask for the definition. A copier you don't know how to unjam? Try to get a real-life demonstration. Security code for a database? Write it down. <u>BUT do all of those things only ONCE.</u> Any of the "how to," "why", "where" or "when" questions are completely acceptable the first time. After that, you can ask and people will answer, but they might be forming opinions about how well you listen and how quickly you learn. <u>Write down the answers so you can reference them:</u> You are going to get a LOT of information and be expected to use it all. Write it down. Keep a small notebook with everything from passcodes to the names of the right people to call for various issues. Keep it with you as much as you can.

Objective	Methodology	Example
How well you understand the overall goals of your team and your organization.	Listen and be aware. Ask.	<u>Listen</u>: Throughout the course of your day, you may overhear conversations and be privy to information that doesn't necessarily have anything to do with you. You don't want to insert yourself and ask what you are hearing means. But you do want to pay attention and see what you can glean about company operations. <u>Ask</u>: Don't put on blinders when it comes to anything having to do with your organization. The more you know, the more you can help, and the more you will get noticed— even if it is not associated directly to your role. **Note:** *Use your judgment if it is something that seems confidential or sensitive, let it go. Don't gossip, but do learn as much as you can about your organization.* For example, let's say you are in a meeting identifying what technical changes need to be made to a software program based on client feedback. Your task may be to write the code to support whatever is decided, but don't zone out when they are discussing client needs. Listen. Be aware and ask, as the more you know, the more you can help and the more you will get noticed.

What To Expect on Your First Day

- Your first day will likely be a lot of paperwork, introductions, and getting settled. Don't lose a lot of sleep about it the night before, because it is unlikely to be particularly stressful.
- People will likely be enthusiastic about meeting you and want to welcome you to the company; they have all had first days. Be sure to take advantage of it because it may not last long.
- Everyone will be busy so don't expect people to be able to spend a lot of time with you. If they do, count yourself lucky and be appreciative.
- There may be a full-scale onboarding process where you are assigned to a mentor and given training on norms and processes, or there may not be.
  - Your mentor may or may not be very interested in helping you. This will have nothing to do with you and a lot to do with how much they have going on.
  - The norms and processes will likely be helpful: ("You need to add a project code when you make copies"), but not comprehensive: ("Here is what it takes to be successful in this role"). Asking questions is a very good idea, and paying careful attention to all that is said and not said is an excellent idea.
- If there is not an onboarding process, and you are "thrown into the deep end" right away, you may need to be aggressive to find
  - your manager,
  - your first assignment,
  - what you are expected to do,
  - a job description,
  - your first assignment,
  - what criteria will be used to judge your first assignment and/ or your job overall,
  - how your manager wants to interact with you. (Weekly status

meetings? Daily phone calls or Zooms? Or on an "as needed" basis?)

Some companies are better than others at onboarding, and the same is true for individual departments and teams. It is not an indication of how good your experience is going to be if your first few days do not go like clockwork, and you should not expect everything to be explained to you in exactly the way you need it, exactly when you need it. It is your responsibility to identify what it is that you need and ask for it. Be patient: You may be coming on board when a big deadline is looming, or the person dedicated to bringing you up-to-speed is going through a personal crisis. Or a hundred other reasons. But be accountable. It is up to you to get all the information you need.

JerseyCoachAmy: *Your first day is going to be way easier than you think it is going to be, even if the job eventually sucks. You mostly fill out forms and meet people. There is really nothing too awful they can do to you right off the bat, so just take a deep breath.*

However, there are a few things that you deserve a clear understanding of in short order and want to request if not offered:

- Your formal job description (the internal one, not the one that was advertised, which usually includes a lot more detail about reporting relationships and requirements for promotion)
- How your performance will be evaluated
- What goals you will be expected to achieve in the short-, medium-, and long-term
- What your relationship with your manager will be like
- Your first set of tasks

Here are some expectations that you may want to adopt for yourself as you become aware of these detailed parameters within your new role:

- If you get documents to read or are asked to familiarize your-self with a model, try to produce something (create an executive summary, make a list of questions, do a little analysis). This will make things more interesting for you, give you a record of some-thing to review, and prove you are a "producer."

- Again, use that small notebook you bought and keep track of the questions you've asked and the answers you've received. As stated in the last section, you can ask as many as you want, but you should only ask them once.

- Keep a file on everything you do—projects, assignments, help-ing others, AND what skills you improved along the way. This will come in very handy at review time when you will need this information in detail.

- Prove you are interested and ready to dive in by asking to meet with a peer or other colleague about the work they are doing. Be respectful and ask for an appointment rather than just starting a conversation.

- Keep an eye out for the unwritten rules of the organization:
  - How much time do people spend chatting? Is it only about work?
  - Is there an expectation that coworkers will eat together?
  - When do you use assistants and for what? How much of your own admin work will you need to do?
  - What is the REAL dress code? No one will say anything to you if you dress inappropriately but most people WILL notice.
  - When is the real time that the people who are the engine of the organization arrive and leave? Again, no one will say anything to you if you get your work done and leave/arrive on your own schedule, but it WILL be noticed. Some organiza-tions really do not mind if you set your own hours, but you

can't make assumptions. You need to find out what the truth is at your firm, virtual or office-based.

Lastly, start off on the right foot by asking how to start contributing immediately. Don't be surprised or upset if it takes a few days for someone to have enough time to bring you up-to-speed on work that is meaningful. In the meantime, take whatever is offered so you can start learning.

A Few Things I Wish I Had Known
(Both JobCoachAmy and JerseyCoachAmy, Contributors)

1. Businesses can be quirky, which makes them both endlessly fascinating—and frustrating.

Businesses may be rooted in numbers and data, but they are operated by humans with personalities and biases and histories and judgment—both good and bad. Work can be exceptionally satisfying in a well-run organization where your objectives are clear and you have what you need to complete your work. It can also be exceptionally frustrating in other conditions. The endlessly fascinating part can come in the gray areas—those times when you are never quite sure what is going to happen next, but you are pretty sure it is going to be, ah, ...interesting.

Be open to learning as much as you can, even when the lessons are hard. The best executives have been through it all and come out the other side.

2. You don't have to compromise your standards to be successful in business.

The example of my cousin, Fred Rich, in Chapter 2 is an example of a real person who is making a real difference in the world. You can also review the career of the much beloved and missed Kevin Landry of TA

Associates to find another example of someone who was wildly successful by any measure. Kevin quietly created an untold number of jobs as both a consistently profitable and beloved private equity investor. He also practiced what a lot of executives only theorize about: a consistent dedication to maintaining the highest ethical standards in his work and personal life. He leaves an incredible legacy in both his family and philanthropy.

3. Jobs are not high school; you are not there to be popular.

You will likely have one job where your colleagues become your family and stay that way long after you've all moved on. Most people, if they're lucky, get one job like that in their lifetime. In most of your jobs, you'll be friends with people at work, but forget each other as soon as you are out the door. You may have one or two jobs where you only like a few people. This information is based on my own, highly anecdotal practices of collecting evidence. All of these situations are fine, and you'll get used to them all. Respect is better than friendship in the workplace.

4. When it comes to senior management decisions, remember, you are not operating with all the information—but they are.

You are going to have management that you respect and management that you do not. Remember that you don't have the same view or the same restrictions from where you are sitting that senior management has from where they are sitting. What seems like a bad decision to you may be the exact same decision you would make if you were in their roles.

5. Ultimately, your soft skills are going to be what gets you to higher ranks.

As your career progresses, try to learn both hard skills (e.g., new software, research and analysis methods, processes) and soft skills (e.g., getting along well with difficult people, when to take initiative, how to rise above poor team dynamics) in equal measure. You'll need both to get ahead.

6. You'll learn quickly that there is no tie between how "smart" you are and how successful you can be.

Intellectual horsepower and business success *can* be linked, but not necessarily. Don't rely on a great academic record to get you very far. Don't be intimidated by someone who comes with a fantastic academic pedigree. Curiosity, hustle, common sense, the ability to learn from mistakes and a lot of other factors make for a good colleague and a rising star at work. These things cannot necessarily be taught.

7. Sometimes you will love your job, and sometimes it will just be a paycheck.

Nobody gets the former all the time, and no one should have that expectation. During the times when your job is just a paycheck, rely on other things in your life to make you happy. The situation won't last forever. If it drags on, use what you have just learned to make a change.

8. You are going to have days when you are just not very productive.

Take those days to do whatever administrivia you have been putting off. Do some filing and some boring paperwork that you've been putting off. Take a lunch break, a real one, and try again. Go to bed early that night. Everyone has those days.

9. Some days and weeks you are going to want to quit.

Don't. If you must, set out a six-month time frame for yourself and start reading job descriptions. If you see something that looks amazing and you can't stop thinking about it, that's a different story. Apply immediately. Just be sure you are running toward something and not away from something.

10. Keep your mouth shut.

If you are wondering whether you can trust someone with personal information or sensitive work information about an account, a colleague, or an upcoming announcement, the answer is always no. It's not worth the potential trouble.

11. Don't go to work sick.

No one wants to be around someone who is contagious. Call in to the meeting. Rest. It's only one day. You'll get better faster instead of dragging it out. You get no points for playing hurt.

12. We are going to need to ask even more from the next generation of women leaders.

The #MeToo movement has shown the world that there is a significant amount of egregious behavior in the corporate world that puts women at a disadvantage, and that we have a very long way to go before there is an even playing field for men and women. This is a really, really good thing. However, an unfortunate side effect will be that a lot of potential male mentors with good intentions for guiding women will drop out because the stakes are too high if their mentorship is misinterpreted. Future Women Leaders, this is going to put a greater burden on you to fill this gap for the women coming up behind you. Coaching and mentorship are important. A shout out to my first coach, George Roser, who in today's day and age would probably not have invested time in a kid that no one was paying much attention to and helped make her a competitor. Thank you.

13. You should not have to compromise if you are willing to work for what you want.

Want to love your work, make a difference in the world, be passionate every day about what you are doing, *and* make enough money to live well and be a generous philanthropist? Sounds impossible. You know it's not, though, if you know my husband, Doug Reeves. He is well-known in the world of K–12 education for his research, consulting, and publishing on professional development and leadership in schools.

Doug has helped a generation of teachers improve the outcomes of school children in some of the poorest school districts in the country. He is a recognized expert in most of the world and a respected professional—someone who is dedicated to his work and truly cares about the students and teachers he helps. His work makes a true difference in the lives of thousands every day—and he checks all the boxes of personal satisfaction along with keeping the highest ethical standards. He works hard. Every day.

What can the average human learn from this kind of example? Whatever it is that sets you apart from the rest of the world exists, and you have a contribution to make because of it. In the same way that there is "an app for that," there is a career for what you can contribute.

I found mine, and you are holding it. What was the biggest disappointment of my life at 22 turned into my strongest inspiration at 49, when I began serving clients as JobCoachAmy. Everything I learned along the way—the good, the bad, and the ugly—is useful for my clients and hopefully for you because I've experienced it myself. My great hope is that it helps flatten for you the learning curves I found steep, short circuits the lessons I found difficult, and leads you towards a career that ultimately brings you joy.

A Few Other Thoughts

Here are a few other thoughts that may help you get started on the right foot:

- Keep an eye on the big picture by following financial and organizational announcements. Try to connect the dots on how what you are doing feeds the organization's success.
- Invest in your peer relationships. If they agree, say, to review your work before you present it, be sure to offer to review theirs. Make sure they know you appreciate their insight and their time.
- Ask for feedback. Generally, if you are doing a good job, people will let you know. If you are not, most managers will avoid telling you—sometimes until it is too late. It is hard to get feedback that is negative, but infinitely better to get it quickly and rectify whatever might be going wrong so that it doesn't impact your formal review.

Summary

- Circle back with people who helped you in your job search: your network, your references, and your friends. If you only call people when you need something, they are much less likely to return your call.
- Understand that your new salary is a privilege and not a right— you have a boss, but so does everyone else up the line, and they are all depending on you. Make sure you know up front how you fit into the big picture and what is expected of you.
- Your new status affords you some opportunities that are only available to new employees: Say hi to everyone, establish good protocols for communicating with your manager, and ask as many questions as you want. But write down the answers so you only need to ask ONCE.

- Make an effort to become known early on as the "go to" person who can be relied upon for high quality work that is produced quickly and thoroughly.
- Do all you can to expedite your learning curve so that people quickly forget you are the new person.
- Show that you understand the overall goals of the team and the organization by asking or talking about your work in a greater context.
- Set up and stick to a consistent communication program with your manager; ask for hard feedback. Managers are people, they don't want to deliver difficult messages. But you don't become the GOAT by just doing your thing and hoping for the best: you get constructive feedback nearly constantly. You want to be appreciative about getting feedback occasionally.

Index

About the Author

Amy Feind Reeves is the Founder and CEO of JobCoachAmy, a Boston-based consultancy where she leverages her experience of over 25 years as a senior executive and hiring manager to help professionals at all levels find and keep jobs that make them happy. She has been featured in the *Wall Street Journal*, *Business Insider*, *The Baltimore Sun*, *Chicago Herald Tribune*, *McMillan Digital*, and Job-Hunt.org. She speaks regularly to undergraduate and alumni groups, women's conferences and at wellness resorts. Amy has an MBA from the Tuck School at Dartmouth College, graduated *cum laude* from Wellesley College and earned a Certificate in Petroleum Engineering from the University of Southwestern Louisiana. She lives in Boston with her family and is a Mendham, New Jersey native.

CPSIA information can be obtained
at www.ICGtesting.com
Printed in the USA
LVHW101252300123
738184LV00006B/190